James Wellard

The Search for the Etruscans

First published in Great Britain in 1973
by Thomas Nelson & Sons Ltd

Copyright © James Wellard 1973

CARDINAL edition first published in 1973
by Sphere Books Ltd, 30/32 Gray's Inn Road,
London WC1X 8JL

This book was designed and produced by
George Rainbird Ltd,
Marble Arch House, 44 Edgware Road, London W2

House editor: Ellen Crampton
Designer: Jonathan Gill-Skelton
Calligraphy and maps: Ieuan Rees

Colour plates originated by
Westerham Press Ltd, Westerham, Kent
Text printed and bound by
Jarrold & Sons Ltd, Norwich

ISBN 0 351 18677 8

In memory of my mother
FRANCES ALICE WELLARD

Small bronze figure of Paris.
The story of Paris and
Aphrodite was a favourite
of the Etruscans.

Contents

Reverse of frontispiece Pan playing the syrinx, or shepherd's pipe. An Etruscan bronze from the 5th century B.C. *Frontispiece* Banquet scene from the Tomb of the Shields, Tarquinia, 330–300 B.C. The Etruscans portrayed in their tombs both the joyful life they knew on earth and the imagined terrors of the Underworld.

Colour Plates

Preface

For reasons which should become clear in the following pages, the study of the Etruscans has tended to be neglected in the English-speaking world. There is, for instance, no Department of Etruscology in any American or British institution of higher learning, so that the serious student of this area of ancient history would have no alternative but to attend a European university for professional instruction. Moreover, while there is a large literature on the subject, a great deal of it is so esoteric that the general reader might well decide that the Etruscans belong to a phase of history best left to the specialists. In consequence, there is considerable popular ignorance as to whom the Etruscans actually were, where they came from, what they contributed to western culture, and why they remain so enigmatic despite all efforts to penetrate the mystery that surrounds them.

In the hope that some of these problems can be clarified, or at least discussed in a comprehensible manner, I have attempted to synthesize what has already been written and, at the same time, to stimulate interest in this strange and fascinating people whose treasures fill the museums of the world.

While researching this wide and complex field of history, I received help from many sources. I wish, therefore, to thank the Trustees of the British Museum for the facilities made available during the writing of this book; the directors of the various museums I visited during my travels in search of the Etruscans; and all those writers whose works are listed in the footnotes and bibliography included in this volume. Special acknowledgment is due to Mr Dennis Rhodes of the Department of Printed Books at the British Museum, whose research is discussed in Chapter Four.

J.W.
September 1972

Etruria and the Etruscans Today

THE ETRUSCANS are one of those mystery peoples of the ancient world who seem to have appeared for a comparatively short while on the stage of history, then to have disappeared altogether. In fact, from the end of the Roman period to the end of the Middle Ages, they could be said to have ceased to exist at all in so far as the sites of their cities, towns, villages, and farms had been completely lost. In this respect one can compare them with the Sumerians, Hittites, Phoenicians, and other even more obscure states which emerged from the hinterland of Asia Minor to establish themselves for a few hundred years as the leaders of civilization in the Mediterranean world, nations whose rise and fall have, of course, been overshadowed by the later empires of Greece and Rome. As for the Etruscans, conventional historians have tended to relegate them to a sort of historical limbo, and this is where one still finds them in the standard textbooks.

Yet during the last two hundred years, these highly civilized and artistic people have, as it were, thrust themselves upon our attention through a sudden outpouring of the treasures they left buried in their tombs, treasures so varied and extensive that national museums all over the world can hardly find room to exhibit them. To these public exhibits should be added an untold number of large and small private collections so that the full extent of Etruscan antiquities has never been assessed, and perhaps never will be. As we shall see, the example of the fantastic looting of the Etruscan places during the last century is a lesson in how men can destroy their own heritage, reducing the civilization of extraordinarily interesting and sympathetic people to the commercial value put upon their artefacts in the auction room. One has only to read the accounts of the nineteenth-century travellers in Tuscany, describing how peasants were employed by princely landowners to break open the tombs and deliberately smash what they regarded as *poca roba* (small stuff), to realize how much of that heritage was destroyed in the frantic search for loot.

Tomb of the Volumnii near Perugia. This magnificent tomb, built in the form of a house, contained seven funerary urns, the most interesting being of a lady called Veilia.

There is, then, an enormous corpus of both Etruscan museum exhibits and books by Etruscologists, so that the interested person can, if he wants, study this people rather as one studies geology or paleontology. If, on the other hand, he wishes to study them as human beings rather than as fossils, he must go back to the land of Etruria, to see if there is some more evocative approach to the proud and vital people who lived there. This is not an easy thing to do in Italy today. It was certainly much easier a hundred, even fifty, years ago when the first seekers after the Etruscans as people and not museum exhibits travelled the lonely roads that led to Tarquinia, Volterra, and Veii. The Etruscan presence could then be felt quite strongly, as the descriptions of these early travellers convincingly show.

And today?

There is a curious and wonderful Etruscan tomb in the hillside beneath the Umbrian town of Perugia, which two thousand five hundred years ago was one of the twelve capitals of the Etruscan Federation. This tomb, once considered the most interesting sepulchre in Italy, was discovered by accident in 1840, and when opened up by the usual pickaxe and shovel methods of those days was found to consist of ten burial chambers, nine of them leading off from the main vault. One of these rooms was a painted tomb, showing the Etruscans at one of their celebrated banquets at which men and their wives or mistresses reclined at table, each with a chaplet round his hair, a torque round his neck, and a wine goblet in his hand. In this main chamber beneath the painting of an eternal revelry was buried the family of the Volumnii, six males and one female of the clan. The names of the men are Larth, Velus, Arnth, and so forth, and they are shown in the effigies on their little sarcophagi as of varying ages, each reclining half-draped on his couch. The lady's name is Veilia, and she is shown as sitting on a throne, surveying the scene like the matriarch she no doubt was in life. Her posture is a hint of what we know was true of the Etruscan culture – that women were not only equal members of society with their husbands and fathers, but enjoyed much the same status that ladies had in the Age of Chivalry. Their liberated condition, in fact, was unique in the ancient world.

Such was the Tomb of the Volumnii a hundred or more years ago, when no traveller passing this way *en route* to Rome omitted to stop along the country road in a landscape of fields and trees typical of the Italy of history and tradition. Its condition today is symptomatic of what the seeker of the Etruscans must expect to find. The railway line and level crossing which pass right beside the mound under which the tomb lies do not interfere with the scene. The constant stream of traffic – heavy lorries, cars driven at maniacal speeds, explosive motorcycles – does, for there is no way of stopping to see the tomb and nobody there to open it up. But what indicates more than anything that the old days of nineteenth-century exploration of Etruria are over is the construction of the new autostrada which will permit travellers to roar by this wonderful site without ever knowing that underneath the huge concrete pylons lie Etruscan patricians amid the rapidly fading scenes of their last revelry, condemned to extinction by the triumph of the new concrete civilization. One sees here in the piles of cement, the huge machines, and the abandoned tomb that a kind of death sentence has been passed on the Etruscans.

ABOVE The temple tombs of Norchia as drawn by George Dennis in 1843. About a hundred of these tombs were sculpted in the cliff face of the valley.

OPPOSITE Three Apulian red-figure vases from Sudbury Hall, Derbyshire, found in 1843 by the 5th Lord Vernon on land he rented at Cumae for the purpose of excavation.

Yet there are still left a few genuine Etruscan places which the traveller who has the time to leave the main roads and a pair of legs to walk with can see, as the early explorers saw them and, indeed, almost as the Etruscans left them. Some of these sites are the most beautiful places in Italy, if not the western world. Norchia, for instance.

The region in which the valley of Norchia lies has been set aside for hunting, as the signs all along the track one follows show. They say *Divieto di caccia*, handwritten on little boards nailed to saplings, and they mean that rich Roman and Milanese industrialists come here in their fast cars to shoot anything in the nature of wildlife that has survived decades of indiscriminate and unseasonal slaughter. One hundred years ago, as the early travellers report, the whole region abounded in game – boars, wolves, bear, and every species of European bird. The last survivors in the springtime are the songbirds. However, in mid-week in early April, the hunters are in their offices, and Norchia becomes one of the loneliest – as it is certainly one of the most enchanting – places in Italy, and a place where it is easy to get lost.

The valley itself is intersected with rapidly running streams overgrown with trees. On either side rise the cliffs in which are sculpted the temple tombs, unique architectural vestiges of the Etruscans. Typical of our ignorance about

13

the Etruscans is the fact that the outside world knew nothing of the existence of these tombs until 1808 when an Italian professor first visited and described them. They have remained almost *terra incognita* from that time onwards, so that it is a strange and impressive experience to come upon them rather as the early explorers came upon Petra, which the tombs of Norchia resemble, for they are really only the façades of temples, with outside columns, pediments, arches, and lintels, and nothing inside. The burial chambers themselves are not within the temples, but are reached by inclined tunnels which lead down on either side of the façade. These chambers are now empty and bare of ornament, and whatever was discovered inside them has been taken away, and no record survives of what was taken. The objects were probably the usual urns and sarcophagi which were placed on stone benches cut into the rock.

It is difficult to say how many of these temple tombs were sculpted in the cliffsides of Norchia – perhaps a hundred or more. So far the site has only been explored by individual antiquarians, beginning with a report made less than one hundred and fifty years ago by the Italian scholar Orioli. But not even the indefatigable George Dennis who visited the valley in 1843 and who did his best to examine as many of the tombs as he could see was able to give a detailed survey of the enormous necropolis. The location of the Etruscan city which must have adjoined this cemetery is also in doubt, though it probably lies on a tongue of land which rises above the ravines. Here one sees the imposing and

Tomb of the Barons, Tarquinia, about 500 B.C. On the left a bearded man with his arm round a boy offers a libation to a woman (a goddess?) at the completion of a horse-race.

romantic ruins of the medieval church and castle of Norchia, and no doubt the Etruscan city stood somewhere on this site, judging from the vestiges of ancient gateways cut through the cliffs. So it would need a well-equipped archaeological team to solve the mystery of Norchia, and if the work is ever to be done, it will have to be done soon, for the majority of the sculpted tombs have now collapsed and fallen down in huge chunks into the valley, the destruction for once not wrought by vandals, but by trees which have thrust their roots down through the tops and sides of the monuments and so split the temples apart. But even though this unique necropolis is now in ruins, the very desolation of the place vividly manifests the essential aura of the Etruscans.

In all the vast territory which the Etruscans once held throughout central and northern Italy, there remain only a few such evocative places as Norchia, and all of them are off the beaten track taken by passers-by on their guided tours. Enough material evidence survives in the form of vases, household articles, weapons, ornaments, and the like – rifled from the tombs by the old excavators (as they called themselves) – to enable the student to gain some idea of their intellectual and artistic achievements. Something of the Etruscan genius can be seen in the magnificent collection of artefacts at the Villa Giulia Museum in Rome and in the celebrated painted tombs at Tarquinia; but the inevitable impression gained from these visits will be that the Etruscans were an enigmatic people who belonged not so much to history as to fable. What is lacking is the sense of their presence – that sense which we feel so strongly in the case of the Greeks, a people we think of as our fellow voyagers on the stream of history. The Etruscans, however, are a people of the shadows. It is in their tombs, or in the halls of museums, that we meet them. And this, of course, is why Etruscology has become such an esoteric and even sterile subject in comparison with the study and appreciation of the Greek, Roman, Egyptian, and Assyrian civilizations, with all of whose cultures we feel a certain *human* affinity.

The experts themselves are involved in endless controversies on many trivial aspects of the Etruscan civilization. It is all the more necessary, therefore, for those who are trying to discover the Etruscans as a living people to begin their search in places like Norchia or anywhere in the Tuscan and Umbrian country-side where one can see from their remains above ground that the Etruscans were a numerous, successful, and vital people who built hundreds of cities, towns, and villages and created an empire which once rivalled that of early Greece and Carthage – all this at a time when Rome was a village of mud huts on the banks of the Tiber.

This search for what we shall call the living Etruscans is not easy to pursue for two reasons. First, we have to remember that Etruria as a nation literally disappeared for some two thousand years, swamped, as it were, by the onrush of history following the conquest of the world by the Romans. Second, Etruria as an empire and a state was annihilated by about 200 B.C., after which it was

George Dennis, author of *Cities and Cemeteries of Etruria*, first published in 1848 and still considered the most valuable and readable book on the subject.

considered by orthodox historians as a kind of backwater in the historical landscape, and so it remained until the sensational discoveries at the end of the eighteenth and beginning of the nineteenth centuries.

As a result of this indifference shown by preceding ages, the Etruria which the first explorers discovered was completely untouched, much of it exactly as the last of the Etruscans left it. There was, it is true, an overlay of Romanization, for after the Romans had conquered the Etruscan cities and reduced their citizens to the status of colonials, they erected their own towers, temples, and theatres, and even renamed the ancient sites. Such a city was Orvieto, which the Romans called Urbs Vetus and whose Etruscan name is not now known at all. Even so, it was once comparatively easy to plot at least the location of scores of Etruscan places, since almost the entire heartland of Etruria itself – that is, the provinces of Tuscany and Umbria – had been largely abandoned from the beginning of the Middle Ages. Thus, from 1842 to 1847 when George Dennis, the greatest of all explorers of Etruria, wandered through these regions of central Italy, he described them as 'almost depopulated by malaria, inhabited by only a few shepherds and husbandmen, and never traversed by the educated and intelligent.'

How different the scene today! Little towns like Cortona, which Dennis found 'squalid in the extreme' and which he remembers as possessing one miserable inn where he was bitten all night by fleas, are now prosperous centres of tourism, smartened up for the annual summer invasion. On the other hand, larger cities like Perugia, which he described as a quiet provincial place, he would not recognize at all; the streets and piazzas through which he wandered looking for relics of Etruscan walls and gates are now so jammed with cars and thronged with people that even the Arco d'Augusto, the great Etruscan-Roman gate which he found so inspiring, can no longer be properly examined, for there is really no place to stop and stare.

What this means is that the Etruria which suddenly reappeared from the malaria-haunted wilderness of nineteenth-century Tuscany and which aroused the wonder of the Victorian world as the immense treasure was brought out of thousands of tombs is now being rapidly submerged under the excrescences of the late twentieth century. Our chances now of finding the essential clues to Etruscan history – where the people came from, what language they spoke, what was their contribution to western culture – are becoming yearly more remote. So the Etruscans may be said still to elude the intensive search of both experts and amateurs to find and identify them, as they eluded the efforts of even their contemporaries. All the same, the search can be just as intriguing today as it was two thousand four hundred years ago when the Greek historian Herodotus first attempted to explain who they were and whence they came.

Sutri, the Etruscan city forty miles north of Rome, as it looked in George Dennis's day.

Part One
The Exploration of Etruria

CHAPTER ONE

The Greek View

W HAT IS SO STRANGE is that we know so much about the Etruscans in some respects, for they left us an abundance of material evidence buried in the ground. We know what they looked like, how they lived, and a great deal about their customs, private and public. We have at least a glimpse of their internal lives. Husbands clasping the hands of their wives look out at us from their monuments, and we look back at them. We can watch them at their favourite games – hunting, wrestling, fishing, or dancing. We even know the names and ages of many of them, what they did in life, and what they expected after death.

Yet they continue to elude us, for despite the enormous amount of scholarship and research which has been devoted to the Etruscans, they seem to become even more remote as time passes, and some of the leading authorities now admit that the ultimate mystery will never be solved. This mystery, of course, is the Etruscan language. We cannot read what they wrote.

While it is true that there are, in any event, very few Etruscan texts for us to read, it is also true that without a knowledge of their literature we cannot expect really to know them as fellow human beings: they tend to remain faceless as well as voiceless, like the Sea People, who are merely a name mentioned by the ancient historians. Yet we see in the case of an even more remote nation, the Sumerians, how the eventual decipherment of their language enabled us to reconstruct the social and political aspects of their civilization and even to share their private thoughts and feelings. Conversely, the loss of the once-voluminous libraries of the Carthaginians means that we know of this remarkable people only through the accounts of them written by their implacable enemies, the Greeks and Romans. It is for this reason that nearly all ancient history is biased, if not outright falsified; and perhaps the same is true of a great deal of modern history. Hence it is that, in general, we accept the Roman historians' opinion that the Carthaginians were a brutal people with whom it was difficult to sympathize; as we accept their frequently stated view that the Etruscans were a lascivious and degenerate nation whose young women obtained a dowry by prostituting themselves. And even if an intelligent and educated Roman refused to accept this charge at its face value, he knew for a fact that Etruscan women were allowed almost the same rights and liberties as men, whereas Roman

Etruscan archway, Viterbo. Conquered by the Romans in 310 B.C., Viterbo's history as an Etruscan city is unknown. Near by are the great temple tombs of Castel d'Asso, Norchia, and Blera.

Terracotta antefix, or roof ornament, probably from an Etruscan temple. It may represent a priestess pouring a libation for a worshipper.

women – if they were respectable, that is – were accorded scarcely any freedom at all. An Etruscan lady was permitted to have her cup of wine at meals and even to pledge her male companion at banquets, as we see in the tomb paintings. A Roman matron of the early Republic, in contrast, was not only not allowed to drink wine in company, but was not allowed to taste that drink at all. Indeed, she was so sharply supervised in this matter that she was never entrusted with the keys to the wine cellar; and prohibition was further enforced by the custom of requiring her to kiss all her husband's male relatives every day with a chaste kiss, right down to second cousins, even if she met one of them by chance in the street. The convention seems to have been a forerunner of our breathalyzer tests. Be that as it may, the Roman historians themselves report a case of a husband killing his wife in the time of Romulus because he caught her drinking wine. He was exonerated in the courts of any crime. And, as late as the first century of our own era, a Roman lady was fined her entire dowry for taking a little wine to settle her stomach. With restrictions like this placed upon women, one can understand why the more bigoted Romans condemned their Etruscan neighbours, particularly as their moral indignation provided them with a justification for continuous wars against the rich Etruscan cities.

What, then, do we know about the Etruscans other than the information vouchsafed us by the Greek and Roman commentators? Who were they? And where did they come from? Characteristically, historians, both ancient and modern, disagree as to their origin and their provenance, and the experts who engage in these arguments have finally admitted that the ensuing polemics have reached a point of complete sterility. This conclusion has been candidly stated by a professional Etruscologist in these words:

> I confess my own ignorance. I do not know who the Etruscans were, nor where they came from, when they arrived in Italy, and if they arrived at all. We appear to have reached a dead end. This is why I like the idea of getting outside help in an attempt to reach a solution. A solution, a real solution, can only be reached if, instead of twisting the limited data we possess in order to adapt them to existing theories, we honestly recognize our own ignorance of the origin of the Etruscans.[1]

What this expert is saying is that the mystery of the origin of the Etruscan is now insoluble, or that it cannot be solved on the basis of the clues now available. But there is nothing to prevent an enthusiast for the Etruscans from re-examining the evidence, particularly that of the language, which is what we shall do in the course of this study.

One begins with the accounts of the contemporaries who, presumably, had access to the records of the Etruscans themselves. Thus, the Greek historian Herodotus, writing in the fifth century B.C. when the Etruscans were masters of central Italy, gives a precise account of the origin of this nation. The Etruscans, he says, were originally natives of Lydia who, because of a long famine, decided

[1] Luisa Banti, 'Della Provenienza degli Etruschi'. *CIBA Foundation Symposium on Medical Biology and Etruscan Origins* (1955), p. 78.

to divide the population into two groups, one group to remain in the homeland under their King, Atys; the other to emigrate under the King's son Tyrrhenos. This latter group marched across country to Smyrna where they built a fleet of boats, loaded them with their valuables, and sailed away in search of a new home. They finally reached the western coast of Italy where they settled during the eighth century B.C.

Herodotus also tells us certain facts about the Lydian-Etruscan character which accord with the evidence of archaeology. He says, for instance, that during the long years of famine which drove them from their original homeland, the Lydians invented a number of dice games in order to spend one day out of two gambling, thus distracting themselves from their hunger. The first day they banqueted. The second day they fasted and gambled; this went on for eighteen years. The story admittedly sounds legendary, but the general picture it gives of the Etruscans as a pleasure-loving people coincides with their own pictures in the painted tombs of the cemeteries.

And so those who accept Herodotus's account of the Lydian homeland of the Etruscans find no difficulty in proving the correctness of this theory; first, because the Greek historian was a contemporary of the people he was writing about; second, because these trans-Mediterranean migrations were characteristic of the first millennium B.C. – witness the exodus of the Greek colonists to southern Italy and of the Phoenicians to North Africa; third, because of the resemblances between Lydian and Etruscan sepulchral architecture; and fourth,

Sarcophagus of a husband and wife, showing the Greek influence on Etruscan portrait sculpture. The *patera*, or libation-dish, held by the man is characteristically Etruscan.

22

because of the oriental mentality of the Etruscans, so different from the stern life view of the Republican Romans. Some commentators would include as additional evidence of the Etruscans' provenance the physiognomy of that people as seen in their facsimiles: the eyes of the married couple on the slab of the sarcophagus found in one of the tombs of Caere are distinctly slanting. Here, however, we are on dangerous ground, for few scholars risk drawing conclusions from this sort of material.

The ancient kingdom of Lydia is situated in western Turkey which, two thousand five hundred years ago, saw the rise of a number of petty principalities whose names are now only memories – Phrygia, Lydia, Caria, Lycia, Pisidia, Pamphylia, and so on. Of these kingdoms Lydia was the most powerful, flourishing as a miniature empire between about 700 and 500 B.C. In its day Sardis, the capital, was a famous city, as its ruins still suggest; and its kings – Gyges, Ardys, Alyattes, and Croesus – still merit a line or two in the history textbooks, particularly the last of them, whose name is a byword for immense wealth. It was this Croesus who, as the ultimate monarch of the Lydian empire, ruled over all of western Asia Minor, receiving tribute from a host of subject peoples and thus acquiring the treasure by which he is remembered. Yet it was this king's misfortunes more than his money which seized the imagination of the classical historians – the fact that a man could be so rich and so unhappy. For of his two sons, the older boy was killed while hunting and the younger was born deaf and hence grew up dumb. And Croesus himself lost his empire to Cyrus the Persian after fourteen years as king (560–546 B.C.) and was apparently burned alive on a funeral pyre as a sacrifice to the victorious Persian gods.

The empire that Croesus inherited and lost was almost the last that we hear of Lydia which, however, had played an important part in the great stream of civilization which rose in the lower Mesopotamian valley in the third millennium B.C., flowed through many channels westward to Greece, and so spread outwards to all the lands bordering the Mediterranean. Lydia was one of these channels, for Sardis was on the Royal Road, or the great East–West highway that joined Mesopotamia with the eastern Mediterranean. Thus political, social, and religious ideas were imported from the East together with the trading goods, and this accounts for the Assyro-Babylonian elements we find in Lydian culture and consequently in Etruscan traditions, assuming that we accept the premise that the two people belonged to the same stock. And when we speak of a culture in the pre-classical world, we must think principally in terms of religion, since all the Asiatic states were theocracies and were ruled in all departments of life by priest-kings and churchmen. If, then, we look at the gods and religious practices of the Lydians, and from them to the Etruscans, we can expect to find an oriental life view which is strongly contrasted with the Greek attitude. Oriental peoples gave total submission to their gods while the Greeks tended to defy theirs.

Herodotus, the 5th-century B.C. Greek historian who first described the Etruscans.

23

At the same time we have to remember that Lydia was a neighbour of the Greek Ionian states whose influence was to be far more dynamic than the conservatism of the declining empires in the East, whence even the gods worshipped by the Lydians underwent a gradual metamorphosis and in the end resembled Aryan more than Semitic deities. The same change is characteristic of the Etruscan pantheon. Most of the principal deities had, as it were, become humanized, which is how they appear in Greek statues – Zeus with his kingly presence, Apollo with his athlete's body, Aphrodite with her sexual fascination. Only in the backwaters of Lydian and Etruscan ritual do we still find the non-Greek concepts – the last reflections of the old nature-gods who had travelled up the Euphrates and the Tigris to Babylonia and Assyria and from there by the great trade routes to Asia Minor.

Perhaps it is in the rituals and religious practices rather than in the nature of the gods that the researcher may find a common denominator for the Lydians and Etruscans, since the plain fact is that the deities of the Middle and Near East, of Asia Minor and the Mediterranean, change their form and merge into one another like raindrops falling into a river. Who can distinguish between the Sumerian Inanna, the Babylonian Ishtar, the Phoenician Astarte, the Hebrew Ashtoreth, the Phrygian and Lydian Cybele, the Greek Aphrodite, the Etruscan Turan, and the Roman Venus? They were all goddesses of love and therefore universal.

But we find specific differences in actual beliefs on the one hand, and in ritual procedures on the other. To primitive people, for instance, there is a great difference between inhumation and cremation, though today we may think of these two methods of disposing of the dead as having no particularly significant religious implications. But both the Lydians and the Etruscans set great store by the manner in which the dead were laid to rest; and one is bound to be struck by the close similarity between their funerary rites – the rock tombs, the vault, the sepulchral couch, the sarcophagus, and, above all, the effigies of husband and wife, hands clasped, reclining on top of their coffin.

Yet, despite the excavations of the American expedition of 1910 to 1914, we still know almost nothing of the Lydian civilization at the time their colonists were supposed to have emigrated to Etruria. Lydia remains a name, as it remained throughout the great days of Greece and Rome, synonymous with luxuriousness and incipient decadence. This view had been originally advanced by Herodotus, who had drawn attention to the custom of Lydian girls prostituting themselves in order to acquire a dowry, though he probably got this wrong, as he did his description of prostitution in Babylon. In both Lydia and Babylon, prostitution was religious in origin, a concomitant of the cult of Astarte, the goddess of fertility. Her rites were attended with manifestations of frenzy brought on by the special music – the soft Lydian airs which were to become famous throughout the Mediterranean world and were always

Male and female dancers, from the Tomb of the Triclinium, Tarquinia. About 470 BC

associated with the flute. It is this characteristic instrument which is depicted on the walls of the painted tombs of Etruria; and it is the sense of abandonment in the orgiastic postures of the dancers which also reminds us of the frenzy of the Lydians under the influence of their hypnotic rhythms. The logical and sceptical Greeks, the rational and uncompromising Romans, were both to express their contempt of this behaviour; and the nineteenth-century moralists who based their ideas of propriety on classical sources were also inclined to be contemptuous of any form of ecstacy, religious or otherwise. Consequently the Etruscans tended to be regarded as innately decadent until that strange genius D. H. Lawrence, who rejected the formality of classicism along with Victorian prudery, presented them in an entirely new light. Lawrence argued that seekers of 'uplift' should go to the Greeks; weight and mass would be provided for those who needed it by the Romans; but lovers of spontaneous life forms – the movement of dancers, 25 the delicate caress between a man and a woman, the laughter of the banquet, the fun of plunging into the sea, all those gay scenes painted on the walls of the Etruscan tombs – should go to the Etruscans.

All this outpouring of Lawrence's own intense belief in surrendering to the senses as opposed to resisting them is, no doubt, quite unacademic and is termed 'belligerent agnosticism' by one Etruscologist; but Lawrence's view does at least vivify a subject which could otherwise be as dry as the dust which is all that is left of the inhabitants of the famous tombs of Tarquinia. For there is no doubt that the picture the sepulchral paintings present to us is often of a people who were frankly sensual and who conceived the perfect existence – as it could only be lived in the hereafter – as consisting of the complete liberation of the senses through feasting, drinking, dancing, and loving. Without knowing much of the formal history of the Etruscans, therefore, Lawrence allowed his intuition to speak for him in his interpretation of the tomb paintings; and his conclusions have, indeed, coloured all subsequent interpretations.

Even so, the story of the Etruscans consists of a great deal more than the visionary outpourings of romanticists: it developed through the hard pedestrian work of generations of scholars, notably from the beginning of the nineteenth century, that great age of exploration, both geographical and intellectual. And so we are bound to come back in the telling of the story to the Etruscans' first historian, Herodotus, with his account of their Lydian origin. If we accept his statement we can think of the immigrants as an oriental people who brought their language and customs to a barbarian Italy in which Rome was still a village of shepherds. More civilized and therefore better organized than their neighbours, the invaders soon established themselves in the most fruitful part of the peninsula as a powerful community – not a nation in the modern sense, but a confederation of independent cities, each of which was a kingdom in its own right.

Yet, by the time of Augustus, seven hundred years after their arrival, Etruria had to all intents ceased to exist; and by the reign of Claudius (A.D. 41–54), who was said to have written an account of them in twenty volumes, the Etruscans had ceased to be a separate and independent people. Though their language and some of their beliefs lingered on in remote corners of Tuscany, they were soon to become a mystery people even to the later Romans. It is no wonder, therefore, that from the end of the classical era to the end of the Middle Ages the Etruscans disappeared from the pages of history, only to be rediscovered in the seventeenth century. From that time onwards the search for them has attracted all manner of amateurs, dilettantes, and eccentrics, to the point, in fact, where professional historians are inclined to dismiss the whole field of Etruscology as 'the playground of cranks'. As we shall see, the quest for the Etruscans is sometimes more diverting than the Etruscans themselves.

CHAPTER TWO

The Renaissance Scholars

THE STUDY of the Etruscans began as a pleasant hobby for country gentlemen with antiquarian interests. Parish priests and provincial scholars living in the old Etruscan territories discovered, during their morning strolls, traces of the vanished race whom they knew about only from classical sources and from occasional ruins which appeared to be pre-Roman. One such Italian gentleman was Giorgio Zanetti, a typical eighteenth-century dilettante, a descendant of Renaissance learning, and consequently able to write about his hobby in a manner which one must not expect to find in the work of the modern expert:

> In the stillness of a calm night, the moon shining brightly, I found myself thinking deeply on the explanations of certain Etruscan letters. A woodland glade just beyond the stream provided me with a delightful walk and here, as I slowly strolled about, I turned over in my mind a thousand thoughts.[1]

But long before G. F. Zanetti had strolled about his woodland glade pondering on the origin of the Etruscan letters (which he concluded, erroneously, were a form of Gothic runes), a Dominican friar called Giovanni Nanni, or Annio of Viterbo, had astounded the learned world by publishing in 1498 a collection of the fragments of the lost works of antiquity which he claimed to have discovered in the archives of Mantua. Among these curious odds and ends of Greek and Latin, the friar included a number of items in the Etruscan language, and it is these items which started the controversy which has been raging ever since. Giovanni Nanni, therefore, is an important name in the history of Etruscology.

Who, then, was this mysterious Dominican friar? He was born in 1432 in the town of Viterbo, which lies about fifty miles north of Rome on the old Via Cassia. Viterbo is in the midst of some of the most interesting and extensive Etruscan settlements, and it is a pleasant place to make one's headquarters. After dark it seems to shut itself off from the outside world behind its medieval walls, and the traveller wandering through its silent streets can imagine Giovanni Nanni at work in one of the old houses overlooking the Cathedral square. A born antiquarian, the friar was fascinated by the history of his native place and, in common with many of his contemporaries, he exerted himself to

[1] G. F. Zanetti, *Nuova Trasfigurazione della lettere Etrusche* ([Venice?], 1751), p. iii.

prove it was historically more important than its rivals. Soon he convinced himself that Viterbo was not a Roman city, even though its name is obviously derived
from the Latin *vetus urbs*. It was, he argued, founded by the Etruscans, the
proof of which was a long inscription affixed in the wall of the Church of St
Angelo in Spata. The inscription, incidentally, is still there, though it is now
weather-worn and neglected. But it repays the effort to read the doggerel Latin,
for it tells of how a damsel called Galiana saved her city from the Roman siege
by appearing naked on the ramparts. At the sight of 'this most beautiful speci-
men of nature', says the plaque, 'the siege was raised. The Romans retired.
Viterbo was saved.' Friar Nanni was properly impressed. It was the sort of
incident which accorded with his view of history.

Very few visitors to Viterbo today read this dedicatory inscription raised in
honour of the Viterbian Helen; and those who do no longer take it literally, as
Giovanni Nanni did, for history is now supposed to be a factual science, whereas
in his day it was a fictional art. In fact, the old friar, who in his obsession to exalt
his native city as not only one of the most historic places in Italy but the very
capital and shrine of ancient Etruria, is alleged by orthodox historians to have
become a forger on an unprecedented scale; and perhaps this is the explanation
of the characteristically vague reports that he was finally poisoned at the orders of
Cesare Borgia. But quite apart from this dubious distinction and from his unorthodox treatment of history, Nanni was a remarkable man in his own right,
renowned for his knowledge of Greek, Latin, Hebrew, and Arabic, and for his
insistence that the Christian world should recommence the Crusades. In
support of his zeal for this holy war, he wrote a book proving that Muhammad
was the true anti-Christ. Such was his method of writing history.

But even more sensational than his religious diatribes was his curious *opus*
entitled *Antiquitatum variarum volumina XVII cum commentariis Fr. Joannis Anii
Viterbensis* (or *Seventeen Books of Extracts from Ancient Authors with a Commentary
by Friar Giovanni Annio of Viterbo*), in which he included fragments of such
obscure writers of antiquity as Archilocus, Berosus the Chaldean, Manetho the
Egyptian, Megasthenes, Q. Fabius Pictor, and others; and inserted among these
spurious fragments several inscriptions in Etruscan. It was no wonder that the
world was astonished by the friar's find, which could be compared in that
classics-oriented age with the discovery of fragments of plays by Shakespeare,
Marlowe, and Ben Jonson in our own times. The *Antiquitatum variarum* went
through many editions until the learned world of the sixteenth century began to
doubt both the honesty of the Dominican and the genuineness of his 'fragments'.
Philippe Cluver, the German antiquarian, pronounced him 'a most impudent
trifler and a nefarious impostor'. George Dennis, first of the British Etruscan
scholars, accused him of having been 'guilty of the foulest of literary crimes . . .
foremost in impudence, unrivalled in voluminous perseverance . . . a wholesale
and crafty forger'. But recently the Swedish scholar, Olaf Danielsson has come

Flute player. Portrait from a
Greek vase ascribed to the
Cleophrades painter (490–
480 B.C.) and found in a
tomb at Vulci. The double
pipes, of Lydian origin, are
frequently depicted in
Etruscan tombs.

OVERLEAF Scene depicting
a lion hunt, from an archaic
Etruscan pitcher. It suggests
the contests between armed
gladiators and wild beasts
later to be staged by the
Romans in their arenas.

to Nanni's defence by maintaining that the friar has been misunderstood and cruelly calumniated. In short, the controversy is still going on; the mystery has not been solved. Did Nanni deliberately forge these fragments of the lost books? Did he actually find a manuscript in the Mantuan archives? Or was he the victim of a hoax?

As for the Etruscan inscriptions he quotes, they appear to be genuine enough, copied as best he could from the walls of tombs, illuminated by a smoky taper, when neither the language nor the alphabet was known. Friar Nanni, after all, was deep in Etruscan country, and close to his native city lay one of the most spectacular cemeteries of southern Etruria, a necropolis, in fact, not dissimilar to the valley of Norchia. One descends to this necropolis, which is known as Castel d'Asso, from the hill on which Viterbo stands and finds oneself in one of those deep ravines which have managed to remain hidden from the passing tourist. The landscape here is still exactly as it was in Friar Nanni's day, and as it was, for that matter, when the Etruscans carved their tombs in the face of the cliffs, conceiving of them as houses along a street. Here they buried their illustrious dead in monumental sepulchres which run for almost a mile along either side of the ravine. Over the false door they often carved the name of the dead person; and it was these epitaphs which the friar may have seen and which he included in his book. Most of these tombs have since been destroyed by the roots of trees and bushes, and only faint traces of the lettering remain. Yet travellers to Castel d'Asso in the first decades of the last century were able to make out words like 'Eca Suthi . . .' which we can translate with a fair degree of certainty as 'This is the tomb of . . .'. Friar Nanni went further than this, and translated all the inscriptions he collected by referring them to Hebrew, which he, along with his contemporaries, regarded as the parent of all languages.

It is not really fair to dismiss this old scholar as an impostor, though Etruscologists today do not take him or his attempts at translating the still-unknown language seriously. He was, of course, a product of his age, which was distinguished by many pedants, eccentrics, and outright charlatans. Indeed, the man who, judging by his strange life, would qualify as the most eccentric of them all turned out to be the founder of the science of Etruscology. He was Thomas Dempster, contemporary of Shakespeare, a Scotsman of whom it was said 'not a day passed that he did not use either his fists or his sword'.

On the first page of his autobiography Dempster announces that he was the twenty-fourth of twenty-nine children and one of triplets at that; and that he learnt the alphabet perfectly in the space of an hour at the age of three. He claims that his grandmother was Eleanor, daughter of the last Stewart Earl of Buchan; his mother, the sister of the Baron of Balquhain; and his father Baron (i.e. Laird) of Muresk, Auchterless, and Killesmont. On the strength of this pedigree, Dempster called himself 'Baron', though it is not certain that he was always believed. In any case, there appears to have been an elder brother, one James,

Sarcophagus of a married couple, from Cerveteri (Caere), dating from about 550 B.C. and now accepted as the work of an Etruscan sculptor. The posture, clothes, and especially the faces of the couple (note the slanting eyes suggesting the Lydian provenance of the Etruscans) make this sculpture one of the great treasures of Etruscan art.

33

heir to the estate and the title. But James decided to marry his father's mistress, Isabella Gordon, and was thereby not unexpectedly disinherited. In revenge, he collected a band of his wife's kinsmen and made an armed attack on his father, who was journeying to one of his estates accompanied by his retinue. A regular battle took place – father Dempster receiving seven bullet wounds in his legs and a sword cut on his head. The would-be parricide, outlawed by royal proclamation, fled to the northern Islands where he engaged in piracy, raiding villages and farms, and even burning the home of the Bishop of Orkney. Having terrorized the countryside for a number of years, James next offered himself as a mercenary in the Low Countries where he met what the old writers called 'a fitting end' – not on the field of battle, but on the garrison square where he was tied to four horses and torn to pieces as the punishment for assaulting a superior officer.

Such was Scotland in the time of Shakespeare, and such were the Scottish aristocrats. The Dempsters were evidently more bloodthirsty and violent than their neighbours, for Thomas, even after he was renowned as a scholar, doctor of laws, professor, and Etruscologist, was notorious throughout Europe as a man who was as ready to draw his sword as his pen. 'He was the terror of all the schoolmasters,' says a contemporary report. Apparently he needed his skill at swordsmanship after he married a lady called Susanna Valeria, for she appears to have been provocative as well as beautiful, judging by this contemporary report:

> In England he met a woman of incomparable beauty, and of an air so noble and graceful that nothing could be more charming, whom he took for his wife. As she was one day seen at Paris, whither Dempster had carried her on his return, and being, as I said, extremely beautiful, and in a most enchanting dress, exposing to public view a neck and breast whiter than the purest snow, such a crowd of people flocked from all sides to see her, that, had not they taken flight in a neighbouring house, it is more than probable they would have been both crushed to death.[1]

Drawings made by William Gell of tombs at Castel d'Asso.

[1] Pierre Bayle, *Dictionnaire Historique et Critique* (Rotterdam: R. Leers, 1st ed. 1697).

34

Rock temples of Castel d'Asso. The façade shows the architecture of an Etruscan house in the 3rd century B.C.

Dempster no doubt had to protect his beautiful wife from individual as well as public attention, but he had such a reputation that few men dared pay open court to Susanna Valeria. For instance, when three officers of the French King's horse guards came to the College of Beauvais in Paris to revenge their young kinsman, whom Dempster had publicly thrashed,[1] Dempster personally led his fellow schoolmasters to the attack, drove the officers up into the belfry of the college, locked them in for several days, and hamstrung their horses.

But despite Dempster's prowess as a swordsman he eventually lost his young wife in Pisa, where he had been appointed professor of Civil Law at the University and commissioned by the Grand Duke of Tuscany to write a book on Etruria. At any rate, Susanna Valeria deserted him in Pisa, seduced, according to the outraged Dempster, by a 'certain Englishman'. It is possible that her husband's habit of reading fourteen hours a day had something to do with his young wife's seeking solace elsewhere though, by all accounts, she could not have found her husband anything but attractive as a man: 'He was tall, above the stature of common man; his hair nearly black and his skin of almost the same colour; his head large, and his bodily aspect altogether kingly; his strength and courage equal to that of any soldier.'

This was Thomas Dempster, the extraordinary man whose scholarship was recognized all over Europe, who escaped the Inquisition, fought scores of duels, was twice deserted by his wife (on the second occasion he chased her and her

[1] 'He caused his breeches to be let down, a lusty fellow to horse him, and whipped him soundly in a full school.' Bayle, *op. cit.*

35

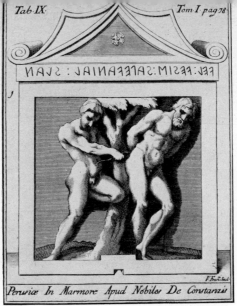

lover as far as the Alps), wrote poems, plays, and a great many learned works (all in Latin, including *De Etruria Regali* and none of them translated into English); he died at the age of forty-six, and was buried in Bologna, far from the Highlands where he was born, the first of a long line of Britons who made the journey to Etruria.

When this extraordinarily pugnacious man found time to study and acquire the immense erudition which made him known throughout all the universities of Europe is puzzling, since he seems never to have stopped travelling from city to city, usually moving on after being expelled on account of his fighting. At the age of sixteen he took first prize in poetry and second in philosophy at the University of Paris. At seventeen he was full professor at the College of Navarre. At eighteen he published a tragedy in Latin called *Stilico*. At nineteen he was a professor of the humanities at Toulouse, where he quarrelled so often and so violently with the authorities that he was forced to resign. Next he turned up at Nîmes where he applied for the professorship of rhetoric, won it at a public exhibition, and then lost his new post for fighting in the streets. And so it went for the remaining score or so years of his life.

His great work, *De Etruria Regali Libri Septem* (Seven Books Concerning the Kingdom of Etruria), was begun in 1616 while he was professor of Civil Law at the University of Pisa and sponsored by Cosimo II, Grand Duke of Tuscany. The book took three years to complete. The manuscript was duly presented to the Duke, but it was not published until over a hundred years later in 1723, when it was printed in Florence at the expense of Thomas Coke, afterwards Earl of Leicester. *De Etruria* is a book of massive scholarship and brings together for the first time almost everything that is known about the Etruscans from the classical historians: that is, their origin, provenance, customs, and history. His early chapters on Etruscan kings, conquests, cities, agriculture, constitution, medicine, religion, and language constitute the starting-point from which all Etruscologists begin their investigations. In Dempster's day the sites of most of

LEFT Cosimo III, Grand Duke of Tuscany, to whom Dempster's *De Etruria* is dedicated. His grandfather, Cosimo II, was the patron of Thomas Dempster.

RIGHT An illustration from *Seven Books Concerning the Kingdom of Etruria* by Thomas Dempster, the founder of Etruscology.

36

A drawing made by the British artist James Byres about 1800 showing an artist at work in an Etruscan tomb.

OVERLEAF Scene from an alabaster urn found at Volterra. A magistrate is being led away by Charun, the Underworld demon with his hammer.

the cities and cemeteries known to us were completely lost, and the actual artefacts were few, whence the Scottish Professor had very little archaeological evidence to help him. There were several collections of vases and bronzes in private museums and from these Dempster gathered examples of the Etruscan language. As a classical scholar he had no difficulty in transliterating the Etruscan names of the gods, and easily recognized Aplu as the Greek Apollo, the Etruscan Menvra as the Latin Minerva, and so on. But he concluded that the Etruscan language was different from both Latin and Greek and followed Annio of Viterbo in ascribing its origin to Hebrew. He gives the first small vocabulary based on glosses found in ancient authors: *arse verse* for *averte ignem* (beware fire), *hister* for *ludio* (actor), and so on. He quotes classical authors to show that the Etruscans were the most advanced people of pre-Roman Italy and that they were actually the originators of institutions and customs which had always been ascribed to the Romans: for example, the wearing of the toga, the office of lictor, the *fasces* as a badge of office, the military triumph, the gladiatorial games, the cultivation of vines and orchards, the war trumpet, the naval vessel, the anchor, and the catapult.

The remainder of Dempster's *magnum opus* is mostly concerned with the geography of Etruria, notably the names and presumed locations of the principal cities, but the information he gives is based on written sources and not on an exploration of the Tuscan countryside. The ruins of Veii, Tarquinii, Caere, Vulci, and scores of other settlements were still unvisited by men of learning, for Dempster's was an age in which scholars believed that the answers to all questions of history could be found either in the classics or in the Bible. It seems then that this much-travelled man never left his library to search for the Etruscan places and so accepted as historical a number of mythical or imaginary towns such as Corythus, Trossuli, Thermae Tauri, and Oropitum, which were mentioned by Roman authors but have not since been identified. All the same, Thomas Dempster laid the foundations upon which all subsequent valid

37

studies of Etruria were to be built, though not much more could be accomplished until archaeology added its evidence to that of the written records.

This evidence was not long in coming forth. In 1728, five years after Dempster's *De Etruria* appeared, excavations were begun at Volterra in consequence of the interest occasioned by its publication. Up to that time, the Etruscan relics which had been turned up by the peasants' ploughs in Tuscany had been smashed and left on the ground, or used as building rubble. In some cases the contents of broken tombs had been left in place, so that when the antiquarians arrived in Volterra to investigate the site, they found scores of urns and vases lying on the ground for the taking. But once the commercial as well as the scholarly value of these finds was recognized, excavations began in earnest and continued uninterrupted for the next thirty years, until the treasure taken out of thousands of tombs in the necropolis to the north of Volterra filled the museums and private collections of all Europe. It was now clear that Volterra, or Velathri as the Etruscans called it, was one of the greatest and wealthiest cities of the ancient world.

The traveller can still see some evidence of this for himself at Volterra, which stands two thousand feet up in the superb hill country of central Tuscany, exactly as the geographer Strabo described it two thousand years ago – 'built on a lofty height, rising from a deep valley, and precipitous on every side'. Modern Volterra, however, is a small provincial town, perhaps only one-fifth of the size of the great metropolis which was encompassed by massive walls five miles in circuit, with towers, temples, and five city gates, one of which survives intact, the celebrated Porto all' Arco. This gate is probably the best remaining example of Etruscan civic architecture; and it has survived for some two thousand five hundred years, though it nearly met its end in 1944 when the Germans decided to demolish it in order to prevent Allied tanks from entering the city. Or so the plaque set up by the citizens of Volterra tells us, adding that the local population protested so vigorously that the German commander agreed to desist from his demolition provided the people blocked up the gateway within twenty four hours. 'Hundreds of citizens,' says the commemorative plaque, 'including women, children, and old men, under the fire of the American artillery, finished the task they had set themselves within a few hours and the Arch was saved.' Weeds sprouting from the wall to which this notice is affixed are beginning to obscure it; in view of the number of German tourists who visit Volterra one can see why nature is being allowed to take its course.

What the tourists – Germans, French, a few English, and fewer Americans – come to see is the Guarnacci Museum which houses the oldest and perhaps the most interesting Etruscan collection in the world. It was presented to his native city by Monsignore Guarnacci in 1761, and even in that day it consisted of so many urns, vases, bronzes, candelabra, mirrors, and other objects from the tombs that it was impossible to display one-hundredth of its treasures, and this

TOP A warrior in his chariot, detail of a bronze cista – a cylindrical box for containing household articles. The artistry and workmanship of this object are proof of the Etruscans' unrivalled skill in the use of bronze.

BOTTOM Painted sarcophagus of an Etruscan noblewoman called Lartie Seianti. The size and splendour of her monument are indicative of the respect shown to women in Etruscan society.

despite the fact that an even greater number of similar objects had been sold by the excavators and antique dealers during the heyday of the Etruscan fashion brought about by the publication of Dempster's *De Etruria*.

But the Guarnacci Museum at Volterra is not just another collection of vases and urns, of interest mainly to specialists in ceramics. On the contrary, the exhibits have a peculiar fascination which D. H. Lawrence has epitomized in his account of his visit to Volterra. For, as the English novelist points out, here are to be seen not the grand 'works of art' that one finds, for instance, in the Etruscan museum at the Villa Giulia in Rome, but a storehouse revealing in a simple, almost rustic, manner the story of everyday life in Etruria. The story is told in sculpture along the front of each little stone sarcophagus, or ash chest, on the lid of which reposes an effigy of the deceased. There are several hundred of these chests, the depositories of the cremated remains of many famous Etruscans who were kings and magistrates in Velathri. Some of them are the memorials of women who were obviously paid the same respect in death as in life, for their urns are just as well made and decorated as those of the leading citizens. There is one marble urn of a young girl, whose frieze shows her studying her lessons in the schoolroom, attended by her teachers. Another of a wife and mother records her last moments on earth: she lies on her death bed surrounded by her family who are shown weeping at the imminence of her departure. These departure scenes are, in fact, characteristic of the Volterra urns, intimating that death for the Etruscans was a journey and not a final ending. The dead are depicted as leaving on this journey on horseback or in covered wagons drawn by four horses. Husbands or wives, children and friends, come to take leave of the traveller. The sense of genuine grief expressed by these unsophisticated carvings is unsurpassed in formal classical art, for we realize that we are looking at ordinary people, not at gods or heroes. An example is the scene on an urn which was the last resting place of a young man who is shown about to start on his journey while his little sister hangs desperately on to the bridle of his horse, hoping to delay his departure. On other urns, husbands and wives embrace for the last time; the man is led away by the angel of death; the woman is comforted by a female spirit. Sometimes the separation is symbolized by a half-open door through which the dead and the living hold hands for the last time. And in some cases, husbands and wives share the same sarcophagus and are shown lying in a loving embrace on the lid, the husband gazing out into some unknown distance, the wife gazing into his eyes.

Not all the scenes sculpted on the ash chests are funereal, however, for some of the deceased obviously preferred to have certain of their achievements or even their pleasures recorded on their monuments. Magistrates are shown on their way to the law courts, wrapped in their togas, preceded by two lictors armed with rods, and followed by court officials carrying legal documents. Victorious generals had their triumphs recorded with a scene of the victory procession –

Medieval square at Viterbo, birthplace of Friar Giovanni Nanni, or Annio (1432–90), one of the first Etruscologists. He was pronounced 'a most impudent trifler and nefarious imposter' by later scholars.

trumpeters, fifers, and harpers in the vanguard, followed by the conquering hero in his gilded chariot. Sportsmen and hunters, too, have appropriate memorials, and we find numerous representations of bullfights, horse-races, gladiatorial combats in the circus arena, and the boar hunts which were evidently a favourite Etruscan pastime. And so to wander through the halls of the museum at Volterra is not the wearisome duty which we so often perform for the improvement of our minds, but a stroll, as it were, through the ancient Etruscan world where schoolgirls attended class, mothers cuddled their children, husbands and wives held hands, and men and their ladies proffered each other a loving cup.

It is no wonder, then, that D. H. Lawrence, with his passionate belief in the senses, found the Guarnacci Museum the most evocative of his Etruscan experiences. Yet in the middle of the eighteenth century, at the time the vast necropolis of Volterra was opened up and thousands of tombs emptied of their contents, these particular urns were considered too plebeian for foreign museums and for collectors, who believed that the only Etruscan artefacts of any value were of Greek origin. And so the more luxurious sarcophagi and vases were sent away to be sold; the rustic ones remained in Volterra. The tombs from which they had come were destroyed and the rubble thrown onto waste heaps. Thus were lost for ever some of the most magnificent sepulchral monuments of antiquity. For example, the Tomb of the Caecina family was looted and completely demolished in 1739. The circular sepulchre, about forty feet in diameter, was found eight feet below the surface of the ground. The entrance to the chamber was closed by a stone slab, and a thick column in the middle of the chamber, which supported the roof, gave an indication of the great age of the tomb. Three tiers of benches were cut out of the living rock, and on these benches had reposed at least forty urns of alabaster, all painted and gilded. Most of these urns had inscriptions in Etruscan, the later ones in Latin. All belonged to the famous family of the Caecina. This tomb, along with thousands of others, has now been lost, and not even its whereabouts is known. The explanation is, of course, that no one in the eighteenth century was particularly interested in the Etruscans as people; so once the tombs had been looted, the ground was ploughed up for cultivation. In short, there was no such thing as archaeology in the modern sense. There was only the 'business' of digging up and selling antiquities.

TOP A scene of leave-taking between husband and wife, with musicians playing (from left to right) a flute, the double pipes, a harp, and a lyre.

BOTTOM Illustration from Dempster's *De Etruria* showing episodes from Greek mythology carved on the sides of a marble sarcophagus.

CHAPTER THREE

The English Pioneers

ONE USES the term 'business' advisedly, for it so happens that the appearance of Thomas Dempster's book coincided with the first excavations at Herculaneum and Pompeii, excavations which were initially sponsored by Charles of Bourbon, King of the Two Sicilies, and carried out for him by army engineers with a plentiful supply of gunpowder and conscript soldiers. The modern archaeologist shudders at the thought of the explosion and pickaxe by which the sappers blasted and hacked their way down through the lava of the eruption which occurred in August of A.D. 79 in order to drag up from the pits and tunnels the treasures of the two buried cities.

Even so, the eighteenth century was an age of great scholarship as well as of taste, a combination which produced those leisurely and discriminating travellers who were wandering about the empires of the ancient world examining the monuments with new eyes. These were the men, compeers of Gibbon and Niebuhr, who were to unearth the lost worlds of Egypt, Mesopotamia, and pre-Roman Italy, discovering them not in libraries but in the lands of their origin. They were, indeed, genuine explorers, even if not in the class of those African travellers who, a century later, were to search for the hidden kingdoms of Negroland and the source of the Nile.

In the eighteenth century, the Near and Middle East, Asia Minor, and even rural Italy were roadless regions, and the curious who wanted to see the ancient places for themselves had to be prepared to undergo considerable hardships. True, journeying to Italy did not present the same dangers as travellers faced in the Middle East and even in Spain, where the roads were unsafe and armed escorts were often necessary between the provincial cities. In Italy, the countryside north of Rome – the ill-famed Maremma, for instance – was hazardous because of the malaria in the trackless regions on either side of the main roads, the squalor of the inns, and the absence of nearly all civilized amenities. Consequently the early explorers of Etruria had to be young and robust, resembling those long-distance hikers who are sometimes met with in the Saharan oases, adventurers driven on by their wanderlust and their interest in primitive places.

Such a man was William Gell (1777–1836) who as soon as he was out of college at the age of twenty was off to the Troad where he made numerous

Sir William Gell (1777–1836) who first described in English the newly discovered Etruscan places.

LEFT The excavations at Pompeii as they looked in 1815.

RIGHT A view of the Temple of Isis, Pompeii.

sketches of the site of Troy. The following year he travelled in Greece and the Aegean and published a report of his travels called *Geography and Antiquities of Ithaca*. His wanderings took him next to Italy, which he explored and wrote about for the benefit of the great wave of English sightseers who were to make the Grand Tour of the Continent in the first half of the nineteenth century. In 1834 appeared his *Topography of Rome and Its Vicinity* which was not only the first guidebook to Italy, but the first report in English of the Etruscan places. William Gell had visited the great necropolis of Tarquinia in 1828 when hundreds of tombs were being opened up, some of them virgin tombs like the celebrated mausoleum called the Grotta Avvolta, which contained the body of a dead Etruscan warrior in gold armour surrounded by his military accoutrements and the customary sepulchral furniture of the Etruscan graves. Nearly all these tombs were covered with paintings, still as fresh and vivid as when they were executed, but nothing had been done to preserve them; and once the tombs had been emptied of their contents, they were left for the peasants to use as sheepfolds or pigsties. Gell also mentions several tumuli which he says resembled the Treasury of Atreus at Mycenae. They were subsequently knocked down to provide rubble for some local building project.

But the greatest loss to the world was undoubtedly the deterioration or outright destruction of the wall paintings whose sociological as well as artistic uniqueness can be gauged from the reproductions made by the British artist James Byres (1772–1817). Byres's drawings were published in London in 1842, in a folio volume entitled *Hypogaei, or Sepulchral Caverns of Tarquinia*; and it is from this publication that we get an idea of the richness of the treasures that the eighteenth-century excavators unearthed and then left to be destroyed in their search for loot. His paintings copied from the Tomb of the Cardinal, for instance, surpassed anything else of their kind in classical art. Indeed, critics have asked whether the copyist has not refined and adapted the originals to suit eighteenth-

47

century taste, for if the Etruscan artists actually did delineate movement in this manner, then they could be compared, as they have been by the Italian scholar Lanzi, with Signorelli and Michelangelo. Their work could also be compared particularly with William Blake's heroic drawings. The portraits of gladiatorial contestants attempting to drive their stilettos into their fallen foe while a third fighter rushes to the rescue of his dying comrade are superb; and so is the vignette of the twin Cupids between the angels of life and death. But most fascinating of all – and the greatest loss to the world since no murals corresponding in interest and beauty can be found today – are the banqueting scenes from a tomb which can no longer be identified. The artist Byres copied four scenes from this lost tomb, each of which shows a man and woman reclining on a raised couch furnished with striped cushions. In the first of these the man wears a chaplet of leaves, the girl a Phrygian bonnet with a little tassel on the end. Both are naked from the waist up. The girl has the hair, profile, and high firm breasts of a young Italian. She rests her hand on the forearm of the man whose hand carries a piece of fruit towards his mouth. They are holding the fruit dish between them and looking at each other with a kind of restrained passion. In attendance on the

ABOVE AND OPPOSITE Views by James Byres of the Tomb of the Cardinal at Tarquinia. His drawing of a gladiatorial contest is shown beneath the same scene as depicted forty years later by Mrs Gray's artist.

OVERLEAF Four banquet scenes from a lost Etruscan tomb, painted by James Byres about 1800. These murals were already nearly destroyed in 1842 when George Dennis visited Tarquinia. Most scholars believe that Byres 'improved' on the originals by adapting the Etruscan style to the mannerisms of 18th-century art.

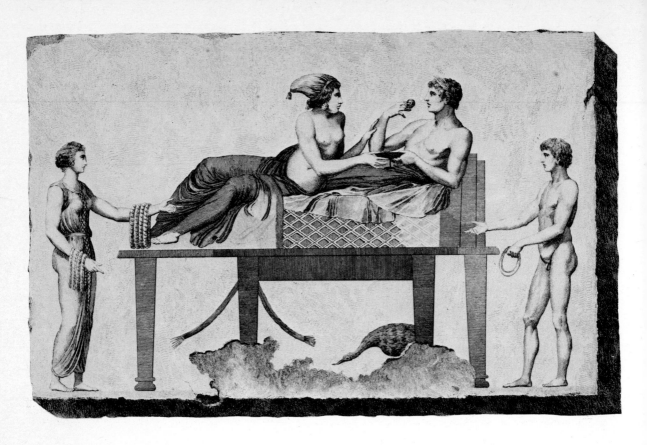

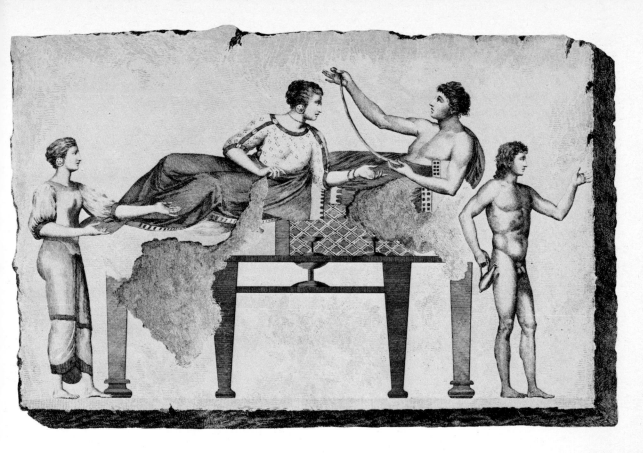

man is a naked boy who holds what appears to be a gold collar. The girl attendant of the woman on the couch is clothed and holds eight chaplets, four on each arm. Underneath the couch, a bird, perhaps a goose, stands with out-stretched neck. It is a picture of tremendous symbolic power and would tell us, if we were sure of its message, a great deal about the life view of the Etruscans. Similarly the other three pictures of the two banqueters are pregnant with mystery. In the second, the girl drinks from a goblet shaped from a ram's head; the man from a flat dish. Both gaze into the distance, dreaming. In this picture and the next the girl is clothed. She could walk into an elegant gathering today in the dress she wore two thousand five hundred years ago, for it consists of a light flowery top decorated with braid at the neck and elbow-length sleeves and a long skirt of darker material. This splendidly clad lady is watching her com-panion hold out for her inspection a snake. In the fourth scene, the girl is elegantly draped but has left one breast bare. She is entertaining her male com-panion with a length of tapestry on which a boar hunt is depicted while he holds his zither and listens to her.

The damage to many of the unique murals was partly due to the smoking torches or flambeaux by the light of which visitors examined them and partly to the smoke of their picnic fires, for it was considered amusing to have supper parties in the tombs. Casual visitors scratched their names on the walls and once the tombs had been emptied of their saleable articles they were abandoned altogether. Literally thousands of them, including many painted tombs, have been thus destroyed.

Even so, it is impossible to estimate the quality and quantity of the treasures wrenched out of the Etruscan soil from the mid-eighteenth to the late nineteenth century, though some idea of the nature and extent of the loot is indicated by the sheer number of the artefacts; one thousand five hundred decorated hand mirrors, for instance, are still extant. The British Museum's collection of bronzes was largely acquired from donations by private collectors who had picked up some of the priceless Etruscan artefacts for a few pounds. Such a collector was the numismatist Richard Payne Knight (1750–1824), an immensely rich man whose wealth enabled him to make a collection of ancient bronzes, coins, and jewels of inestimable beauty and value. His bequest to the British Museum formed the basis of that institution's collection of Etruscan bronzes.

A cultivated dilettante like Richard Payne Knight was, of course, an aesthete who valued a work of art for its beauty, not merely for its market price. Very different were the landowners who regarded their buried treasure as though it were a gold or silver mine, to be dug until the rich vein gave out. The most ruthless of these tradesmen in antiquities was undoubtedly Lucien Bonaparte (1775–1840), Prince of Canino and brother of Napoleon.

The principality of Canino had been sold in 1814 by the Pope to Lucien Bonaparte and survives as a village some forty miles north-west of Rome in the

Lucien Bonaparte, brother of Napoleon and Prince of Canino, who excavated the necropolis of Vulci in 1820. More antiquities were discovered there than at any other site in the ancient world.

LEFT A drawing of a
bronze mirror from Sir
William Betham's
Etruria Celtica. This one
was among the finds of
Lucien Bonaparte.

RIGHT A gold ornament
from Todi, found in the
same tomb as the necklace
on page 60.

heart of Etruscan country. An English traveller, Mrs Hamilton Gray made a pilgrimage there in 1839, calling at the Prince's home, or country seat, at Musignano. She apparently had high hopes of meeting Lucien Bonaparte himself, for she was one of those rather endearing Victorian snobs who do not conceal their passion for titles. Unfortunately, neither the Prince nor his chaplain, Father Maurizio, who was in charge of the Etruscan collection, was in residence, and the English visitor was shown around the Musignano museum by the bailiff who had been summoned, obviously to his disgust, from getting on with the running of the estate. Mrs Gray's reciprocal annoyance is characteristically expressed in this fashion: 'We regretted exceedingly that we were so unfortunate as not to meet the Padre Maurizio, from whose politeness and learning we should have had the most perfect information, which we were unable to extract from the rustic whom the computista sent to attend us.'[1]

Mrs Gray was shown a collection of vases which did not impress her: 'The clay itself was coarse, and the style of art did not surpass mediocrity.' What, no doubt, she really would have liked to see – as any woman would – were the gold and jewelled ornaments worn by the Princess of Canino, the widow Jouberthou, at the ambassadors' fêtes in Rome, decorations 'which were the envy of society and excelled the *chefs d'œuvres* of Paris or Vienna'. Indeed, these priceless orna-ments were not untypical of the treasures Lucien Bonaparte had been taking out of the tombs on his estate for twenty years – a collection of artefacts unique in the history of excavations. We no longer have a complete record of what this land-owner found in his rape of scores of the tombs, but he amassed enough vases, bronzes, ornaments, weapons, and utensils of all kinds to provide sizeable

[1] Mrs Elizabeth Caroline
Hamilton Gray, *Tour to the
Sepulchres of Etruria* (London:
J. Hatchard and Son, 1840),
pp. 278, 279.

Etruscan collections for kings, princes, prelates, nobles, landowners, and even private individuals of modest means all over Europe. A contemporary of the Prince of Canino declares that the necropolis of Vulci, which was Lucien Bonaparte's principal treasure trove, had yielded more antiquities than any other site in the ancient world, not excepting, in certain respects, Herculaneum or Pompeii.

Yet such is the mystery still enshrouding the Etruscans that Vulci itself is scarcely mentioned by Roman writers and the site of the metropolis whose citizens were buried in such numbers and in such splendour is not even visible. Until the 1820s, in fact, the existence of the great cemetery was completely unknown and it was only discovered, as so many other subterranean treasure houses were, by accident. It appears that the ground suddenly gave way beneath a peasant who was ploughing, and on hearing about the discovery of vases and other relics in the tomb thus revealed, the Prince of Canino undertook personal direction of the digging and *within four months, in a plot of ground not more than four acres in extent, brought out from the subterranean tombs over two thousand Etruscan artefacts.* Landowners of adjacent properties now joined in the search and all were quickly and richly rewarded. All that was required was to open the tombs and carry out the contents for disposal by the dealers in Rome, Florence, and other Italian cities. George Dennis, who visited Chiusi in 1844, speaks of half a dozen titled dealers in Etruscan artefacts and mentions an 'antique supermarket' in the high street. He found the prices very moderate.

We are given an eyewitness account of the methods the landowners employed by Dennis, who in 1843 witnessed the opening of a grave at Vulci by a gang of excavators.[1] At the top of the pit stood the overseer, with his gun beside him – a reminder to the peasants not to try and secrete anything of value on their persons. Inside the pit, the labourers were busy shovelling out earth from a tomb whose roof had collapsed and half filled the chamber below with soil which had to be removed in order to get at any articles which might be lying on the shelves and the floor of the tomb. In the case of this particular tomb, the diggers quickly got down to ground level and passed up a hoard of pottery, coarse and unvarnished, but elegantly turned, and thus pointing to a very early period of Etruscan history. Everything that came out of the tomb was deliberately smashed to pieces by the workmen and ground beneath the heels of their boots on command of the overseer: his orders were to destroy everything that struck him as of no special pecuniary value on the Rome antique market, and he would not even allow Dennis to keep one of the black-ware or *bucchero* vases as a souvenir. The entire contents of this ancient tomb were thus destroyed within a few minutes and the tomb itself, now turned into a crumbling ruin, filled in with earth and rubble. This procedure was repeated at each of the tombs where the finds were assessed as unlikely to fetch a good price. The potential supply was nevertheless enormous, since at least six thousand tombs were reputed to have been opened in the necropolis of Vulci alone.

In 1890 when the French archaeologist Stéphane Gsell was invited by Prince Torlonia (who had acquired the estate from the Bonapartes) to make a survey of the site, only some hundred tombs were identifiable; yet so many tombs had

Ponte della Badia, an Etrusco-Roman bridge near the necropolis of Vulci. The stalactites suggest that an aqueduct once crossed the bridge.

[1] George Dennis, *Cities and Cemeteries of Etruria* (London: Dent, Everyman's Library, 1907), vol. I, pp. 431 ff.

been opened that approximately nine out of ten of the Etruscan vases now extant come from Vulci; and it is estimated that the site, though worked for almost one hundred and fifty years, would still yield artefacts of interest to the modern archaeologist, if not to the treasure hunter.

A visit to the site of Vulci today is a rather melancholy experience, though the countryside is green and sunlit even in early April. It used to be one of the districts in central Italy most plagued by malaria, and the early travellers describe it as a desert. There were no houses or farms for miles thereabouts, and the only landmark was the medieval castle, garrisoned in the nineteenth century by a few customs officers. The castle is still there, inhabited by a custodian and his wife, neither of whom will put in an appearance if the visitor arrives during the sacred siesta period between one and three o'clock. But one has no need of a guide at Vulci. The massive castle tells its own story as does the famous Ponte della Badia, the Etrusco-Roman bridge which still spans the Fiora River at the bottom of the ravine. The stalactites which excited the wonder of all the travellers who visited this spot still depend from the sides of this venerable bridge, suggesting that it was once crossed by an aqueduct built, no doubt, by the Romans. The buttresses of the Ponte della Badia are constructed of the huge blocks of tufo with which the Etruscans built their public monuments, the upper parts with the dressed stone employed by the Romans. The roadway itself is medieval, so the bridge represents the work of three eras in history and has stood there for two thousand five hundred years.

The city and necropolis of Vulci remain almost as lost as they were until Lucien Bonaparte's peasant accidentally opened up a tomb in 1828. The city itself was apparently situated about a mile below the bridge, but there are no

LEFT A vessel for wine or oil, with a ram's head at one end and a spout at the other. The geometric design of the decoration indicates its great age.

RIGHT A bronze incense burner in the form of a dancing girl. 7th–6th century B.C.

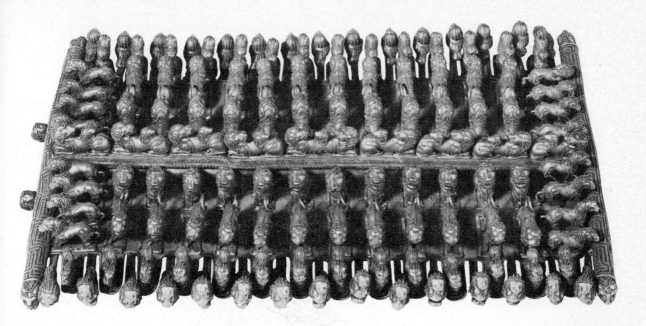

A 7th-century B.C. gold clasp, approximately 4⅝ inches by 6⅞ inches, from the Barberini tomb at Palestrina. The rows of tiny figures probably represent orientalized lions and horses.

traces of it apart from fragments of its walls. The curious fact is that while the city appears to have been a relatively small Etruscan centre and is not even mentioned by the ancient writers, the size of its cemetery and the enormous treasure taken out of its tombs indicated that it must have been a populous and wealthy metropolis. But the problems and mysteries of Vulci are typical of our ignorance of the Etruscans, and the seeker after the truth will get little help from a visit to the site itself. Only two of the hundreds of tombs rifled by the nineteenth-century landowners are now open, though the visitor will have to try and find the custodian with the keys if he wants to see inside them. One of these sepulchres is the Isis Tomb whose unique treasures were acquired by the British Museum in 1850.

The contents of the tombs, then, were saved if they had value in the antique market. But gradually the educated public began to take an interest in Etruria not merely as a source of antiquity but as an integral part of western civilization. Early private collectors concentrated on the more elegant vases made in the Greek ateliers or produced in Etruria according to Greek design and workmanship while a few discerning scholars saw the importance of the older and more primitive artefacts as the expression of the native genius. In England this interest was due to two nineteenth-century travellers, neither of whom was a professional historian. The first of them was Elizabeth Caroline Hamilton Gray.

Mrs Gray was the wife of the Reverend John Hamilton Gray, who was given the living of the parish of Bolsover, near Chesterfield, in Derbyshire; and she tells us that the first time she saw the incumbent whom her husband was replacing, this gentleman was running off as hard as he could carrying a pail of water. He was running because a woman was chasing him with a carving knife and he was carrying the water to throw at his assailant in case she caught him. The woman was the vicar's wife. Such was the parish of Bolsover, where the church had a congregation of six, the churchwarden's daughter was the local tart, and 'drunkenness was reckoned good company and unchastity a common and very excusable misfortune'. Not unexpectedly, Mrs Hamilton Gray, whose health was supposed to be 'delicate', was glad to be ordered to winter in Italy; and it was during her sojourn there that she began her Etruscan studies at the Archaeological Society of Rome and accompanied the walking classes which were led by the German scholars, Professor Nibby and Dr Emile Braun.

In the month of February 1839, she tells us,[1] a Roman dealer in antiquities invited her to be present at the opening of a tomb at Veii, the once-splendid Etruscan neighbour of Rome, which had been annihilated by its rival after almost a century of war. Mrs Gray's excursion to the site of the Etruscan city was typical of early nineteenth-century archaeology; it was as much a social as a scientific event, as those involved, including the professors, saw no reason why digging up the past should not be a festive occasion. One recalls the Babylonian excavations of the British Consul Claudius J. Rich in Mesopotamia at the beginning of the nineteenth century, when this brilliant young foreign officer who helped establish the science of Assyriology rode out from Baghdad with his guests, picnic baskets, and small private army to sketch the landscape and burrow into the mounds of the lost cities.[2]

Mrs Gray and her party rode out to the site of Veii where 'the ground is hired out to the different dealers and antiquaries in Rome.' She arrived in time for the opening of a tomb and being the only foreign lady in the company was invited by the Italian excavator to enter the subterranean chamber first. She writes:

> The workmen made a few steps of the earth they had turned out, and I leaped down to the bottom after their pickaxes had removed the stones from the main door. I entered the tomb, a single chamber arched in the rock, apparently ten or twelve feet square, and somewhat low; it was so dark that I was obliged to have a torch, which a labourer held within the door that I might see by myself what was the arrangement of the tomb and what it contained.[3]

Evidently she was disappointed at the loot thus revealed, and so no doubt was the dealer in antiquities, for the tomb contained about twenty vases of various shapes and sizes, all of the most primitive sort, and all scattered about the floor. There was nothing else – no sarcophagus, though the place was marked where one had stood; no gold, no bronze, no figures in stone or clay, and no marbles.

Still, this was a risk the treasure hunters took, for they were by no means the first who had broken into the Etruscan tombs and carried off anything unusual, throwing the funerary vases and furniture onto the floor and stripping the dead of their ornaments. Mrs Gray's party took their disappointment in good spirits, for they had had an interesting excursion, and, as a reward for their enterprise, were allowed to divide the findings of the tomb among themselves as 'more

Designs from an Etruscan vase depicting a procession of priests and the marking out of a new city's limits by an ox-drawn plough. The drawings were made by the 19th-century German Etruscologist, Edouard Gerhard.

[1] Gray, op. cit. (2nd ed., 1841), pp. 79 ff.
[2] See James Wellard, By the Waters of Babylon (London: Hutchinson, 1972), Ch. 3. Published in the United States as Babylon (New York: Saturday Review Press, 1972).
[3] Gray, op. cit. (2nd ed., 1841), p. 81.

memorials of the day than as articles of any worth'. The Englishwoman's low opinion of the sixth-century B.C. vase which she received as her share of the find explains the enormous number of Etruscan artefacts, especially pots of every size and description, still found in private homes all over Europe. Most of these articles were acquired by travellers for a few shillings on their Italian tour, sometimes from peasants in the Etruscan towns, sometimes from antique dealers in Florence or Rome. The first-comers, like Mrs Hamilton Gray, were allowed to help themselves where a tomb which had already been rifled yielded up, as she implies, articles of little worth. Genuine Etruscan *objets d'art* can still, in fact, be bought in Rome or Florence, though reproductions are naturally more numerous as business in antiques booms.

In Mrs Gray's day, Etruscan excavations were in the main carried out by commercial speculators, hired as agents of the families who owned the land in which the ancient cities and cemeteries lay buried. For instance, after her experience of a dig at Veii, Mrs Gray went on another of the walking classes, this time to Monteroni near Cerveteri (ancient Caere) and met the Duchess of Sermoneta, described as 'a woman of great spirit', whose *contadini* were hacking their way through the tumuli on her estate, but finding nothing of any particular value according to the antiquarian standards of the time. But had she known it, the Duchess was digging into one of the oldest and most interesting sites in Etruria, dating back perhaps to the period of the original kings of that nation. True, her excavators had high expectations when they started breaking into a tumulus about forty feet high, for they guessed that this mound must have been man-made from the low basement wall which surrounded it. In fact, they found a cylinder in this wall which later archaeologists recognized as a marker pointing to the tunnel leading to the sepulchral chamber in the heart of the mound. Ignorant of the nature of this cylinder, the workmen sank holes in the surface of the tumulus until they struck a passage cut into the rock which led to a small tomb. The excavators were disappointed, however, at what they found, which was some *bucchero* or black-ware pottery, a few vases ornamented with lotus flowers, beads of glass and amber, and ostrich eggs. None of these finds were of any interest to the antique dealers, so the Duchess, after opening several other tombs which were honeycombed with lateral and perpendicular passages like the Egyptian pyramids, suspended her treasure hunt, the unique mounds of Monteroni were more or less levelled with the ground for agricultural purposes, and a few years later nothing was to be seen that told of their existence.

If, however, the Duchess of Sermoneta had continued her excavations, she might with luck have stumbled upon the site of the great Etruscan port of Pyrgi at near-by Santa Severa, the port which served the great cities of the southern confederation – Caere, Veii, Sutri, and others. It was known from the classical authors that one of the most famous temples of the ancient world stood on the shores of the Mediterranean at Pyrgi, a shrine endowed with gold and silver,

Gold necklace with triple-plaited chain and pendants, from a 4th-century B.C. Etruscan tomb near Todi in Umbria. Similar gold and jewelled ornaments were worn by Lucien Bonaparte's wife 'the widow Jouberthou', at embassy functions in Rome.

61

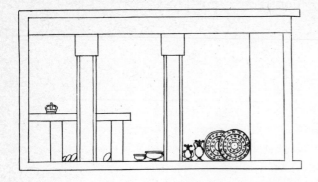
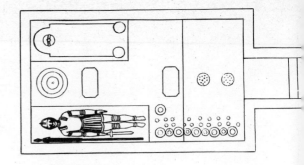

the gifts of Etruscan cities to the goddess Uni, the Astarte of the Carthaginians. On the other hand, without the sophisticated skills of modern archaeology the Duchess's workmen could not have found, as the Italian team working on the site between 1957 and 1971 found, the actual site of this temple, including the dedicatory plaque of beaten gold, proclaiming in the Punic and Etruscan languages the erection of the sacred shrine by King Velianas, one of the most exciting finds of recent archaeology.

It is not surprising, then, that Mrs Hamilton Gray was disappointed with her visit to the Cerite territory, since it left her with very little to report, though she manages to fill a few blank pages in her narrative with reflections on the vanity of human wishes.

Journeying next northwards to Tarquinia, she was better rewarded for her enthusiasm, for Tarquinia when the English lady visited it in 1839 had become one of Europe's most fascinating archaeological centres. This was not as a result of any scientific exploration of the site, but of an accident involving a certain Carlo Avvolta, the chief magistrate of Tarquinia, who in 1823 was digging into a mound for stones to mend a road, when he opened a hole in the roof of an Etruscan tomb and peering down saw a man in full armour stretched out on a rock, with a crown of gold on his head and a sword by his side. Then, as the Magistrate gazed on this extraordinary sight, the 'body became agitated with a sort of trembling, heaving motion (which lasted a few minutes) and then quickly disappeared, dissolved by contact with the air.' Avvolta scrambled into this virgin tomb as soon as he could, for he realised that he had made the haul of a lifetime. In addition to the crown, the tomb contained burnt bones and scraps of the warrior's woollen garment; a lance and eight javelins placed by his side; a two-edged, cross-hilted sword on the couch, placed in the hand of the deceased; two bronze circular shields; urn-shaped bronze pitchers; and rows of terracotta vases of various shapes and sizes – in brief, the funerary collection intended for a royal personage's sojourn in the next world. The greatest treasure of this tomb was, of course, the crown of gold which was made up of very fine sheets of the precious metal affixed to a bronze plate and sculpted with lilies in relief – evidently a fantastically beautiful example of Etruscan

ABOVE AND OPPOSITE
Illustrations from Mrs Hamilton Gray's *Tour to the Sepulchres of Etruria*. Drawings of the tomb (now lost) discovered in 1823 by Carlo Avvolta which contained a warrior in full armour with a golden crown; and a Grecian-type wine cup presented to Mrs Gray on her visit to Tarquinia.

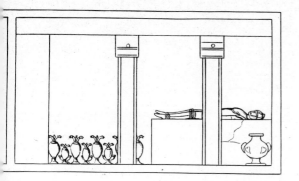

metal-work. What happened to this diadem? 'It perished utterly in its journey to Rome owing to the oxydization of the bronze,' says George Dennis, 'save a small portion which passed into Lord Kinnaird's possession.'[1]

Mrs Gray happened to meet the celebrated magistrate Avvolta on her visit to Tarquinia, for when her party arrived they found the inn full and a lodging in the near-by Bruschi Palace unacceptable in view of the appearance of the *padrone*, 'a man whose unprepossessing exterior was not improved by intoxica-tion'. Signor Avvolta was therefore hastily summoned; the other travellers were ejected from the inn and the Gray party was ensconced.

It is not necessary to follow Mrs Gray much farther in her wanderings since her descriptions of the Etruscan places are inclined to be tedious as well as inaccurate and evidently caused great annoyance to her successor, George Dennis, who finally loses patience and describes her as possessing too much imagination. In fact, he says, Mrs Gray's vivid imagination led her to describe the statue of a seated female exhibited in a private collection in Chiusi as 'the most beautiful and solemn manner of embellishing death that ever entered a mortal's head'. 'Nonsense!' remarks Dennis. 'I could only see in it a caricature of humanity.'[2]

However, Mrs Gray did actually see and describe a number of the painted tombs before the colours had begun to fade, and she picked up odds and ends of information which are still fascinating to the Etruscologist. She reports, for instance, that two thousand tombs had been opened and plundered between 1823 and 1839 and that these two thousand were only a few of those estimated to form the vast necropolis of Tarquinia. She also informs us that the paintings had already so far decayed in her day (1839) that they bore little resemblance to the copies of them that were made when the tombs were first opened only a dozen or so years previously. She also gives an account of several Etruscan inscriptions which have since disappeared, though her rendering of the texts is ludicrous and made more so by her pompous statement that she cannot explain them 'without bringing forward more learning than will be acceptable to the general reader, but I will make them so simple and intelligible as I can'.[3] Her method of simplifying the Etruscan is to identify the original words with any

[1] Dennis, *op. cit.*, vol. I, p. 395.
[2] Dennis, *op. cit.*, vol. II, pp. 294–5.
[3] Gray, *op. cit.* (2nd ed., 1841), p. 179.

language that happens to resemble them – whether it be Latin, Greek, or Hebrew. Thus she transliterates one Etruscan phrase into *cives Ana*, which she then proceeds to translate as 'Citizen Ana – a priestess'. A word she reads as *Eura* she says comes from the Hebrew meaning 'glory'. *Chuacha* is the same as χοαί χεάσται 'offerings to the dead'. It was all, of course, guesswork and a great deal of it outright nonsense yet, at the same time, so typical of subsequent Etruscan studies that we can ill afford to feel superior to this earnest English-woman who, as Dennis himself observes, 'is deserving of all praise for having first introduced Etruria to the notice of her countrymen'. Certainly Mrs Gray did her best to describe the wonder and beauties of the Etruscan cemeteries which she visited and to include in her book reproductions in colour of a number of tomb paintings. It is apparent, however, that her artist romanticized the scenes he was required to paint and considerable efforts were made to spare Victorian feelings where nakedness was concerned. None the less, her repro-ductions and descriptions are, in some cases, all that we have left of the murals which were allowed to deteriorate once the tombs had been opened and the contents sold. To her credit, Mrs Gray repeatedly drew the attention of her readers to what was happening to the superb paintings, particularly in the most magnificent of all the Tarquinian tombs – that called the Grotta Querciola, considered by many to be the most beautiful monument of all Etruria. George Dennis agrees with her as to the disaster which was overtaking the Querciola

Drawings by an unknown artist made for Mrs Gray's book: ABOVE Scenes from the Tomb of the Triclinium showing, on the main wall, a banquet in progress and, on the side walls, scenes of music and dancing. OPPOSITE Similar scenes from the Tomb of the Boar Hunt.

Tomb, though he disagrees with her description of the content and meaning of the murals. Referring to one of the scenes in which a girl seated at a table is throwing her arms round the neck of her male companion, he notes:

> Gerhard makes her an honest woman and the wife of her feast-fellow. Mrs. Gray, with a praiseworthy tenderness of her sex, is blind to the evident amorous *abandon* of this fair Etruscan and can see in her only 'an afflicted mother consoled by her remaining son.'[1]

In spite of its drawbacks, however, Mrs Gray's book went through several editions, proving that there was a lively interest in this hitherto arcane subject.

It is now apparent that Mrs Gray's successor in the Etruscan field, George Dennis, was a very different type of traveller. The clergyman's wife, after all, was restricted by the conventions of her time and station, and it is fruitless to criticize her for either her opinions or her sentiments. George Dennis, on the other hand, was one of those free souls who transcend his age and his age's fashions, and in this he can be compared with his contemporaries, Henry Layard and Richard Burton. In fact, Dennis is to Etruria what Layard was to Assyria and Burton to Arabia. All three were great explorers, though George Dennis of Etruria was, for reasons we shall discuss, largely ignored during his lifetime and wholly forgotten after his death.

[1] Dennis, *op. cit.*, vol. I, p. 323, fn. 3.

CHAPTER FOUR

The Founder of English Etruscology

GEORGE DENNIS was born in 1814 and died eighty-four years later in 1898, so his active life spanned almost the entire Victorian era. While he was in many respects what his contemporaries would have called 'an honest Christian gentleman', he was worlds apart from that stereotype associated with the top-hatted, frock-coated *pater-familias* of Victorian melodrama. Certainly that is not the impression we get of him from reading his books. The impression we do get is that of a resourceful and amusing traveller, full of wit and wisdom, missing nothing of interest, including a pretty face: a man we would choose for a companion on a long journey.

But biographical facts about this remarkable explorer were almost non-existent until Dennis Rhodes,[1] a bibliographer at the British Museum, undertook the enormous research required to find out even the simplest data concerning Dennis – such as whether or not he was married and had children. For despite his remarkable achievements, Dennis's name is not even listed in the *Dictionary of National Biography*.

George Dennis left school when he was fifteen. He never attended university, and this makes his scholarship and intellectual achievements all the more remarkable, for he taught himself to read the classics, both Greek and Latin, in the original. He later added French, Spanish, Portuguese, Italian, Modern Greek, Turkish, and a little Arabic to his repertoire of languages. In this extraordinary aptitude for learning languages and mastering the new discoveries in history, anthropology, and archaeology, he resembled those other great Victorian explorers, Rawlinson, Layard, and Burton, all of them non-academics who none the less contributed much to formal scholarship. He was typical, too, of his age and generation in that he worked alone, with nothing more than token help from the academics or an occasional financial grant from the museums who benefited by the priceless antiques that he acquired for them. Finally, we get a glimpse of the characteristic intellectual and physical resources of the man from reading that, as a lad, George Dennis thought nothing of walking forty miles a day through the mountains of Scotland and Wales.

At the age of twenty-two, he was wandering about Portugal and Spain and writing a book of travels which he called *A Summer in Andalucia*. It is still, like

[1] It can be said that everything that is now known about George Dennis has been discovered by Mr Rhodes and will be found in his book, *Dennis of Etruria*, which is awaiting publication. In the meantime, the author has generously permitted me to read his manuscript and to make use of the relevant facts in it.

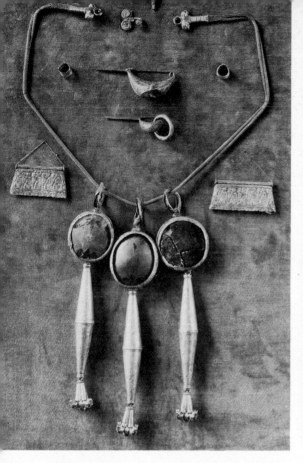

LEFT Jewellery such as these pieces, made by Etruscan goldsmiths and found in the unrifled tombs at Vulci, was greatly coveted by 19th-century ladies.

RIGHT George Dennis as an old man. He is wearing his decoration as a Companion of the Order of St Michael and St George.

all his writings, a very readable book, with a brilliant and moving description of a bullfight, which he found horrible. So by the time he was twenty-five, with considerable travel behind him and a book already published, George's mind was made up. He was determined to be an explorer, which did not mean what it means today – a member of a well-organized scientific expedition – but a solitary traveller who was alone responsible for where he went and what happened to him. The least of his hardships were the villainous inns in which he could expect to be devoured by fleas and bedbugs. In Madrid, Dennis wrote, 'Here, as everywhere else in Spain, I am devoured by bugs of gigantic proportions.'

There were, however, compensations which Dennis certainly appreciated. Returning to Madrid on the top of a coach, he spent the night lying on a feather bed with 'no companion but a young lady who shared the mattress with me and talked and sung to me all the night long'. But in keeping with the decorum of the time, talking and singing were all that did take place between these two young people. Restraint under such circumstances must have been difficult for George, since it is obvious from his comments that he was fond of women, as they must have been of him. Perhaps that is why his father wrote to him, when he was setting out on his Etruscan explorations in 1842 at the age of twenty-eight, not to 'look at the French beauties, even at *Arles*'.

But for the next six years, when he was riding and tramping through Etruria, 67

ABOVE Layard of Nineveh, the brilliant Assyriologist who befriended George Dennis.

OPPOSITE A funerary *cippus*, or column, decorated with scenes of a young lyre-player (left) and a young dancer (right), both shown between two adults. About 580 B.C.

George Dennis was to have little time to look at girls, except the passing glances he gave and no doubt received from the daughters of innkeepers in the depth of the Italian countryside. In those days – the mid-nineteenth century – the country immediately beyond the walls of Rome and the provincial towns was sparsely populated and even uninhabited, a landscape of dense forests, semi-deserted villages, and abandoned or lost Etruscan cities. It was for this reason that anyone who ventured into the trackless and uncharted country of the Tuscan Maremma was a genuine explorer, as this description of a shepherd's cabin situated *not more than ten miles from the centre of Rome*, shows:

> It is a curious sight – the interior of a *capanna* – and affords an agreeable diversity to the antiquity-hunter. A little boldness is requisite to pass through the pack of dogs, white as new-dropt lambs, but large and fierce as wolves which, were the shepherd not at hand, would tear in pieces whoever might venture to approach the hut. . . . In this hut lived twenty-five men, their nether limbs clad in goat-skins, with the hair outwards, realizing the satyrs of ancient fable: but they had no nymphs to tease, nor shepherdesses to woo. . . . They were a band of celibates, without vows. In such huts they dwell all the year round, flaying lambs, or shearing sheep, living on bread, ricotta, and water, very rarely tasting meat or wine, and sleeping on shelves ranged round the hut, like berths in a ship's cabin. Thus are the dreams of Arcadia dispelled by realities![1]

The realities today are of a very different sort, so much so that there is no resemblance between the Italy which Dennis describes and that same country less than one hundred and fifty years later. The Roman *campagna* has been largely destroyed, and those who knew Rome itself even twenty years ago can see that the world's capital is suffering the same fate. The nature of these developments is significant for the future of Etruria and of Etruscology, since the great centres of the old civilizations become lost for ever under the weight of roads, factories, and new towns, and Dennis's shepherds strike us as being archaic as the rustics of Theocritus. To this extent we should be grateful for the record left us by the author of *Cities and Cemeteries* and the sketches made by his companion, Samuel Ainsley, who accompanied him on some of the tours. One is again reminded of other young men of the time who set out on their travels to un-charted regions – Henry Layard, for instance, who at about the same time that Dennis was wandering through Italy with Samuel Ainsley had set out on his journey through Asia Minor accompanied by his artist friend, Edward Mitford. It was such adventurers who gave us our last glimpse of the classical and medieval worlds and contributed to the magnificent discoveries of the Victorian era. Today one would hardly compare travel in Italy with travel in Iraq from the point of view of tourist facilities, but in Dennis's time there was not all that much difference between his journeys in Tuscany and Layard's in Meso-potamia. Consider, for instance, his description of an Etruscan site called Castel d'Asso, some forty-five miles north of Rome:

[1] George Dennis, *Cities and Cemeteries of Etruria* (London: Dent, Everyman's Library, 1907), vol. I, pp. 99–100.

We were now on the great Etruscan plain which was here and there darkened by wood, but unenlivened by towns or villages; no habitations visible on its vast expanse save the distant towers of Toscanella, and a lonely farm-house or crumbling ruin studding its surface at wide intervals. . . . presently [we] came upon the object of our search. Tomb after tomb, hewn out of the cliffs, on either hand – a street of sepulchres; all with a strong house-like character! They were unlike any Etruscan tombs I had yet seen – hewn into square architectural façades, with bold cornices and mouldings in high relief, and many inscriptions graven on their fronts in the striking characters and mysterious language of Etruria. I can well understand the impressive effect such a scene is calculated to produce on a sensitive mind: the solemnity of the site, the loneliness, seclusion, and utter stillness of the scene – the absence of all habitation – nothing but the ruined and picturesque castle on the opposite precipice and the grand dark mass of the Ciminian looking down on the glen.[1]

Of course, not all the Etruscan sites that Dennis visited were as remote and lonely as Castel d'Asso, for many of them were, and are, in the vicinity of provincial towns like Viterbo, Tarquinia, Orvieto, and Siena. But time has changed the character of these places almost beyond recognition, and Dennis's comments concerning the inns and the innkeepers, the local clergy and butchers and shepherds whom he met read like descriptions of travel in medieval England. And as in medieval England, the hardships along the route were not so much due to physical danger from bandits, footpads, and the like (Dennis always regarded these menaces – whether in Spain, Italy, North Africa, or Turkey – as an ordinary fact of life), but from the meanness of the inns, the lack of a decent meal at the end of a long day's exploration, and the near impossibility of a night's rest on account of the fleas and bedbugs. But it was because the young Englishman was prepared to go hungry and often sleepless that he was the actual discoverer of several lost Etruscan sites, notably Sovana, fifty miles north of Tarquinia, a city which flourished perhaps between the eighth and sixth centuries B.C., after which date it was not only abandoned but completely lost until Dennis and Ainsley stumbled upon it. The former was therefore justified in remarking that:

In a country almost depopulated by malaria, inhabited only by shepherds and husbandmen, and never traversed by the educated and intelligent, the most striking monuments may remain for ages unnoticed.[2]

Despite his discoveries, Dennis received little recognition outside of the interest shown by a few German scholars in Rome. Even an article describing his findings that he wrote for an English journal was not only never published but was eventually lost. This withholding of his rightful recognition as a pioneer archaeologist all through his active lifetime was to be continued even after his death.

Yet George Dennis's masterpiece, *Cities and Cemeteries of Etruria*, was in its way as monumental an achievement as Henry Layard's *Nineveh and its Remains*,

[1] Dennis, *op. cit.*, vol. I, pp. 274–5.
[2] Dennis, *op. cit.*, vol. I, p. 493.

George Dennis's sketch of cliffside tombs at Castel d'Asso, which he visited in 1842.

though it brought him nothing like the financial rewards and fame that – rightly – came to the Assyriologist. In fact, immediately after the publication of his *magnum opus*, Dennis was obliged to think about a career which was to take him far from his beloved Etruscans. He entered the Colonial Service and was posted to British Guiana, where he spent the next fourteen years. What this exile meant to a scholar of his attainments is revealed in a letter to his publisher, John Murray:

> Politics, sugar, rum, and the weather (not to mention scandal) are the staples of conversation. . . . There is not a man in the colony (barring the Governor) who cares for literature. It is a dreary residence for one that loveth the lands of old. My Genius must have been irate when he cast my lot in the far West. I hope he soon intends to transfer me to a fairer land than this region of mud, molasses, and musquitoes. I envy Layard returned to the East to bring Nineveh to light. If there were a chance of such occupation for me, I would return incontinently.[1]

Indeed, in his continuous attempts to escape from 'the mud and steam of Demarara', he began in a pathetically humble manner to ask Layard to intervene

[1] Dennis Rhodes, *Dennis of Etruria* (see note on page 66).

The Campana Tomb at Veii, as illustrated in Dennis's *Cities and Cemeteries* and shown 'as it was discovered'. The bones on the funerary slabs are those of an unnamed man and his wife.

for him with Lord John Russell, the Foreign Secretary, whom he dared not approach personally.

In 1863, when he was nearly fifty years old, George Dennis was finally released from what had become a term of imprisonment. He was, incidentally, now married, though – as with the rest of his life story – we know almost nothing about his wife; even her maiden name is unknown, and so is the actual date of their wedding. All we know of Mrs Dennis is that she accompanied him on all his subsequent travels, which took him as Vice-Consul first to Sicily, then to Benghazi, and then to Smyrna in western Turkey. Here we leave him now an old man of nearly seventy, digging in the ruins of Sardis, the capital of ancient Lydia, still searching for clues of the original Etruscan homeland which no one has yet been able to establish.

Dennis's *Cities and Cemeteries* was published in a second and revised edition during his lifetime and it sold modestly well until the end of the century, though nothing like Layard's *Nineveh*. Poor Dennis, while he was always sincerely grateful to Layard who was a true friend to him, was none the less human enough to envy that celebrated man's success. He writes:

> In those early days [he is speaking of 1839 and writing nearly fifty years later when he was seventy-three] we were on a level, both having to make our way in the world, but he, though after wonderful vicissitudes and adventures, has risen far above me, who remain a hack in official harness to the last, while he has won the Derby.[1]

1 Dennis Rhodes, *Dennis of Etruria* (see note on page 66).

On the other hand, Dennis did receive some acclaim and in his last years was accepted by the *cognoscenti* as a great archaeologist of the mid-nineteenth-century variety: that is, a lone explorer in a field not before worked over by academic historians. When he was seventy-one, his few admirers arranged for him to receive an honorary Doctorate of Civil Law at Oxford. It was, of course, a great honour for a man who was entirely self-taught, except for an elementary grounding in the classical languages. The only other distinction granted him after a lifetime devoted to public service and selfless scholarship was his creation as a Companion of the Order of St Michael and St George. Henry Layard, in contrast, crowned his career as an archaeologist by being appointed successively Under-Secretary for Foreign Affairs, Privy Councillor, Envoy Extraordinary to Madrid, and Ambassador at Constantinople.

What, one wonders, are the reasons for this curious lack of appreciation of Dennis's work. Not only has the man himself been almost wholly forgotten but his book, a model of a certain genre of English classic, went out of print with the 1907 edition which had appeared that year as an item in the Everyman's Library. Its editor's introduction gave not a single fact about the author. *Cities*

A sketch made by George Dennis of one of the six hundred tumuli which existed in his day (1843) at Tarquinia. Most of these mounds have since been destroyed.

and Cemeteries is now unobtainable except in the larger libraries or, by a stroke of luck, from second-hand booksellers. Perhaps one reason for the neglect becomes evident from a reading of the contemporary criticisms and opinions concerning the author. They are summed up in Professor A. H. Sayce's review on the occasion of the publication of the second edition of *Cities and Cemeteries*: 'Mr Dennis does not profess to solve any problems whatsoever. He is rather the genial and learned guide of the intelligent traveller, the enthusiastic historian of Etruscan greatness and culture, the agreeable companion of the drawing-room and the library.' Nothing, of course, could be more certain to discredit the work of a layman in the eyes of the academicians than the adjectives 'genial', 'enthusiastic', and 'agreeable'. They represent a sort of pat on the back for a good try. And one suspects that since Dennis was regarded as a dilettante, without any authorization from the schools to devote himself to a subject as arcane as the Etruscans, the professional historians did not altogether approve of him or his methods, precisely as they disapproved of Edward Gibbon who, like Dennis, was an amateur. It is hardly surprising that in the world of nineteenth-century scholarship, dominated as it was by German formalism, Dennis was damned with faint praise.

Yet his history of Etruria (like Gibbon's *Decline and Fall of the Roman Empire*) can hardly be faulted and remains, after almost one hundred and fifty years of continuous Etruscan studies, by far the most comprehensive textbook we have on the subject. But it is more than that. It is written with the enthusiasm of a young man brimming with energy, fun, and the spirit of adventure. While never losing sight of his subject and never padding, he manages to describe an Italy which is as vivid to the reader today as it was in 1842, though we must not expect to see those shepherds with their goat-skin leggings, nor the rustic inns where he teased the buxom hostesses.

George Dennis died in London, apparently alone. His death certificate lists 'Senile decay. Rigors after use of catheter. Seven day's exhaustion.' He was buried without ceremony in the suburban cemetery of West Hampstead, leaving an estate of just under two thousand pounds and no descendants. The only public memorial to his name is over the gateway of a little Italian town called Ferento. The plaque is in Italian and was put up fifty years ago not by his own countrymen, but by the Department of Roman Antiquities of the Italian Ministry of Public Works.

CHAPTER FIVE

Sir Richard Burton and D. H. Lawrence

I T WOULD NOT, of course, be correct to imply that George Dennis was friendless and wholly ignored during his lifetime. On the contrary, he always had many friends, though perhaps acquaintances would be a more accurate term. Among them were most of the archaeological explorers of the period, particularly those who were wandering about in Asia Minor when Dennis was consul at Smyrna in Turkey. They included Heinrich Schliemann, Sir Charles Wilson, James Fergusson, Professor William Ramsay, and Salomon Reinach: to all of these celebrated scholars Dennis played host or guide. Another of his acquaintances was Richard Francis Burton, who met Dennis on two occasions, once in Venice and once in Palermo, Sicily. But whereas Burton calls Dennis 'My friend and colleague' (and then proceeds to misquote the title of his 'friend's' book, calling it *Cities and Cemeteries of Western Etruria*), Dennis has this to say of Burton:

> I don't feel at all honoured by being booked as his friend. I only saw him once for five minutes when he called on me in Palermo. He came to my back door, looked at my Arab horses, and was off. There is friendship![1]

Nor did Dennis think much of Burton's book, *Etruscan Bologna: a Study*, published in 1876. This volume bears all the signs of having been written by a man in a hurry – and by one who had merely taken up the Etruscans in passing. In fact, during his consulship at Trieste from 1871 onwards, Burton used to make occasional dashes around Italy in between his longer excursions to India, Egypt, and West Africa. For, though he was now fifty and his great discoveries in Arabia and Africa were behind him, this brilliant and restless man had by no means lost his fascination with travel, and not even the tropical diseases from which he now suffered could keep him immobile in the safe, comfortable, and dull confines of his consular post. And so when he had no more exciting expeditions on hand, he explored the ancient monuments of Istria and the Etruscan antiquities of northern Italy. The result of these excursions was his *Etruscan Bologna*, one of the least known of his many publications, and under-standably so, for it is an extremely pedestrian book, only enlivened by occasional flashes of his typical sardonic humour.

What contribution then, if any, did Burton make to Etruscology? He was,

[1] Dennis Rhodes, *Dennis of Etruria* (see note on page 66).

after all, an anthropologist and linguist of exceptional brilliance whose immense knowledge of races and languages might have added something new and interesting to the work done by George Dennis, particularly in the difficult area of the Etruscan language. But his curious decision to use up almost half of his study in cataloguing the antiquities in the Bologna museums was not likely to produce a readable book, while his enthusiasm for the then fashionable science of craniology, to which he devotes many pages in his book, reads today as so much bogus scholarship. Anthropological theories based upon 'zygomatic arches, the auditory meatus, and the mandible', sound suspiciously like the jargon of those phrenologists who used to read people's heads at fairgrounds.

But Richard Burton did make one remarkable contribution to Etruscology, even though at the time he did not realize the significance of his discovery and, in fact, never lived to learn what a unique and indeed invaluable Etruscan artefact had slipped through his hands. For Burton was the first man to draw the English-speaking world's attention to that strange object called the Zagreb mummy, which was to affect drastically all future studies of the Etruscans. For the Zagreb mummy was not simply the embalmed corpse, wrapped in the traditional linen bands, of a red-headed Egyptian girl. The linen itself was covered with an unknown script which Burton saw, studied, but never recognized as a unique example of an Etruscan manuscript. The Zagreb mummy is central to the story of the search for the Etruscans, while at the same time it typifies, in its way, the strange vicissitudes of the science of Etruscology.

The Egyptian relic was acquired in Alexandria in 1848 by a Croatian called Michael Baric, a minor official in the Hungarian Chancellery. While travelling in Egypt, Baric bought as a souvenir a sarcophagus containing (he hoped) a mummy. There was, at this time, a very brisk trade in mummies, either for the interest attached to the actual coffins in which they were enclosed, or for the ornaments which were sometimes found on the cadaver. In earlier times still, the embalmed bodies of ancient Egyptians had an additional value; they were ground up and used as medicine – 'mummy' being a staple drug found in all well-stocked apothecaries' shops throughout Europe. 'Mummy' was said to be especially effective for wounds, bruises, varicose veins, and dysentery, the discovery of its curative properties being ascribed to the celebrated Jewish physician, El Magar, who lived in Alexandria in the twelfth century.

But by the mid-nineteenth century when Michael Baric obtained his relic, 'mummy' was no longer in general use as a medicine, and the buying and selling of the corpses was restricted to antiquarians and tourists. The latter group were often palmed off with a fake. The English mummy expert, Thomas Joseph Pettigrew, a surgeon at the Charing Cross Hospital and at the Asylum for Female Orphans, reports many cases where innocent travellers brought back from Egypt bundles of rubbish consisting of sawdust, rags, sticks, the vertebrae of cats, monkey bones, and the like, stuffed into bogus sarcophagi made in the

Head of Achelous, the river god. Late 6th- or early 5th-century bronze, provenance unknown, but probably from a Tarquinian tomb where similar masks were placed near the deceased, possibly as a charm to keep away evil spirits.

76

back streets of the Cairo bazaars. One wonders if specimens of these frauds are not still reposing in the minor museums and private collections of the western world.

But Baric was lucky, for he had acquired a genuine sarcophagus and mummy, though neither he nor any one else for the next fifty years had any idea of the unique nature of his purchase. Still, even to have one's own mummy in the 1840s was something of an achievement, and excitement was always great when the relic was presented to the public at a special ceremony known as 'opening the mummy'. Thus, a huge sarcophagus brought back from Thebes by the French traveller M. Cailliaud was opened in Paris in the presence of learned men on 30 November 1823, and after the seven layers of wrappings were unwound, making some six hundred yards of linen two to three inches wide, the savants found themselves face to face with a naked man fifty to fifty-five years old, his arms and hands held straight against his sides, his hair, which was perfectly preserved, being lightly marcelled, his chest, arms, and belly flecked with the remains of gilt. But what was most interesting of all to the scholars was the discovery that the wrappings round this mummy were inscribed in Greek. As we shall see, the linen bindings of Michael Baric's mummy were even more sensational.

He was not to know this, however, for he died in 1859, bequeathing his souvenir to his brother Elias, a parish priest of a village in Slavonia. Elias had even less interest in this object than his brother Michael, who had at least had some fun by standing his souvenir upright in the corner of his drawing-room and informing his credulous lady visitors that it was the body of the sister of King Stephen of Hungary. Elias preferred to get rid of the mummy altogether and so he presented it to the museum of Agram (today Zagreb) where it was duly catalogued as follows:

> Mummy of a young woman (with wrappings removed) standing in a glass case and held upright by an iron rod. Another glass case contains the mummy's bandages which are completely covered with writing in an unknown and hitherto undeciphered language, representing an outstanding treasure of the National Museum.

The existence of the mummy with the unknown writing on the wrappings was first reported in an article in *The Croatian Review* of 1880, but it had already come to the attention of Richard Burton in 1877. Burton had published his *Etruscan Bologna* in the previous year. During his exile, this extraordinary man, in addition to his interest in the Etruscans, had commenced a study of runes in the hope of finding a connection between the runic alphabet and the Arabian script of el-Mushajjar; and while travelling to Alexandria in the company of Dr Heinrich Brugsch, the greatest Egyptologist of his time, Burton happened to be discussing his theory of the origin of runes, when Dr Brugsch remarked that the runic script reminded him of the writing he had found on the wrappings

TOP Tumulus at Cerveteri (Caere) in the necropolis of Banditaccia. Cerveteri is one of the few Etruscan sites which was not demolished by 19th-century 'excavators' and its massive tombs look today much as they did when George Dennis visited the Etruscan city in the 1840s.

BOTTOM Tomb of the Reliefs, Cerveteri. A 4th-century B.C. burial chamber decorated with stucco facsimiles of household utensils. The tomb represents a room in an Etruscan house, with a sloping ceiling, central beam, and supporting pillars.

of the Zagreb mummy ten years before. 'Imagine my surprise,' the German doctor remarked, 'when I found that the characters were not hieroglyphs, but partly Greco-European and partly Runic; at any rate, non-Egyptian.'

Brugsch and Burton both concluded that the unknown text was a translation of the Egyptian Book of the Dead into some Arabic tongue. Both, of course, were wrong, though to Burton goes the distinction of being the first to get the text copied out for publication and study. At his suggestion, Mrs Burton requested Philip Proby Cautley, the Vice-Consul, to undertake the onerous and difficult job of copying the text.

In January of 1878, therefore, Vice-Consul Cautley presented himself at the Zagreb Museum where he was cordially received by the Director, the abbé Ljubic. The mummy still stood in the museum, but the bandages had been removed to the abbé's study, where Cautley inspected them. The Vice-Consul now makes a significant comment in his report to Burton, for he says:

> The writing is divided into sections of five or six lines each, measuring about seven and a half inches long, according to the length of the cloth. These must have been in hundreds; and one of the best specimens was shown to me at the town photographer's. Each piece appears to have been a chapter . . .[1]

Now if Philip Cautley is saying that there must have been *hundreds* of lengths of bandages inscribed with Etruscan script (one of which had evidently been acquired by the local photographer), it is possible, and indeed even probable, that a considerable amount of the original has gone astray by being passed round among the interested citizens of Zagreb and hence has, by this time, been

LEFT D. H. Lawrence (1885–1930) whose *Etruscan Places*, written as a result of his travels in Tuscany in 1927, presented the Etruscans in a new light.

RIGHT Richard Burton, who in 1887 discovered the Zagreb mummy, an embalmed corpse wrapped in linen bands covered with Etruscan writing – the only Etruscan manuscript that has come down to us.

[1] Richard F. Burton, 'The Ogham Runes and El-Mushajjar: a Study', *Transactions of the Royal Society of Literature*, vol. XII, No. 1 (1882), pp. 32–8.

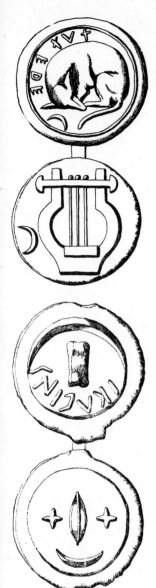

So-called Etruscan coins used by Sir William Betham, the Irish Etruscologist, in an attempt to prove that the Etruscan and Irish languages were related.

lost. Additional evidence for this theory is Burton's statement that, according to Dr Brugsch who examined the bandages in 1867, the number of lines would have filled sixty octavo pages. At thirty lines to a page, this would amount to one thousand eight hundred lines. What we actually have are some two hundred and sixteen lines.

Cautley now persuaded the abbé Ljubic to let him try copying the text on tracing cloth, an idea which 'seemed to excite the priest's merriment'. Nevertheless, the Vice-Consul worked away and was able to copy five chapters of five or six lines each of the now famous *liber linteus*, a sample of which was first given to the world in 1882 in the *Transactions of the Royal Society of Literature*.

It is astonishing that Burton's discovery – in its way as significant as his African findings – was ignored or passed over by European scholars, since Cautley's tracings represented the first piece of Etruscan literature ever to be seen since Roman times. Moreover, every piece of Etruscan script that had come to light had always presented the possibility that the experts might finally find the key to the language and so an answer to the many puzzles of this mysterious people. But not a single scholar throughout Europe recognized the text of the Zagreb mummy as Etruscan, even though this was a period of intensive research into the unknown language by some of the greatest philologists of the time.

There are several reasons. First, the *Transactions of the Royal Society of Literature* could not be expected to have had a very large circulation outside the actual membership of the Society itself; second, Richard Burton's linguistic theory of an oriental origin of the Ogham runes was never taken seriously by the academicians, who probably ignored his article; and third, Cautley's tracings are not very precise, whence it is difficult even for someone familiar with the Etruscan alphabet to recognize the script as it is reproduced in the twelfth volume of the *Transactions*. In fact, it took another ten years for the Etruscologists to realize that the most important philological find of the century awaited them in the Zagreb Museum.

It was the Germans who eventually solved the mystery of the Zagreb mummy, since it was the nineteenth-century German scholars who undoubtedly had the necessary erudition and methodology to do so. There was certainly not a single British Etruscologist of any stature at this time. In fact, the subject has never appealed to British scholars, though it has always fascinated erudite amateurs like George Dennis; and it has always attracted devoted eccentrics like Sir William Betham, who spent many a happy hour (as Burton no doubt did with his palm runes) translating – or, rather, torturing – Etruscan into English by means of a key of his own invention. The Sir William Bethams, indeed, are still with us, and hardly a year passes that some amateur does not 'solve' the mystery.

But as one would expect, there was no nonsense about the Germans' approach to the Zagreb mummy. In 1891, they obtained permission from the authorities

81

for the actual bandages to be sent to the library of the University of Vienna where Professor Jakob Krall was able to make his examination under laboratory conditions, with the help and advice of his learned colleagues. It was not long before he suspected the Etruscan origin of the text, not only by recognizing the alphabet but by identifying several words whose meaning had been guessed at or was actually known from ancient glosses. His surprise was great, however, for he had expected the script to be either Coptic, Libyan, or Carian, so now the question of forgery arose. Admittedly, the likelihood of some prankster amusing himself by covering yards of linen with Etruscan characters seemed remote, but stranger things have happened in the world of scholarship, as the Piltdown skull will constantly remind us. The Germans were taking no chances of being hoaxed, so the professors set about analysing the linen bandages, the ink, and all the circumstances involved in the mummy. They proved conclusively that the wrappings were genuine Egyptian mummy bandages of the Greco-Roman period and that the ink was made in the ancient manner from soot or pulverized coal. Hence the forger, if such there was, would have had to go to great pains to find or manufacture the genuine articles. In any case, the number and variety of words which were not known at the time (1891) but were found in inscriptions unearthed at a later date proved beyond a doubt that the text must have been written by an Etruscan scribe.

The next question that required an answer was whether the inscribed bandages had been specially prepared for the dead girl as her personal shroud; or whether they were bandages which the embalmers had acquired at a remnants sale. Egyptian morticians obviously needed enormous quantities of linen for swaddling their corpses and they were not particular about where it came from. We may compare the wrapping in a contemporary newspaper of some frangible object like a teacup for export abroad. The archaeologist of the future would probably be more puzzled by the newspaper than by the cup. The Egyptian embalmers, however, were not interested in what, if anything, was written on the linen they tore into strips to make bandages for swaddling the mummy, and Professor Krall believed from his examination of the Zagreb bandages that this was the explanation of the Etruscan text; for he concluded that the linen on which the text was originally written was torn into strips rather recklessly, without consideration for the proper sequence of the lines. Moreover, the strips were bound round the mummy with the writing facing inwards, which would imply that whatever it said had no reference to the dead person.

There are, then, two theories to choose from. The first is that the dead girl was herself an Etruscan who died in Egypt where she may have lived with her family. In common with other foreigners who died in Alexandria, she was embalmed before burial. The Etruscan part of the ceremony in that case would have been the inclusion of a memorial of some kind, and that is what the *liber linteus* must be. This theory has been accepted by those scholars who maintain that many

An alabaster funerary urn from Volterra in which the woman holds a piece of fruit instead of the customary libation dish.

82

rich Etruscan families fled to Egypt after the conquest of their principal cities by the Romans during the Republic – a diaspora which could, perhaps, be compared with the exodus of Jews from Germany to America during the 1930s. Also comparable with the Jewish migration would be the Etruscans' devotion to their own religion and their own gods, about which the mummy book seems to be primarily concerned.

But here difficulties arise; for if the text on the bandages is a book of ritual, as most Etruscologists now take for granted, why was it wrapped round the body of a young woman? We know from the evidence of other mummies that the custom was then (as it is now) to commemorate the deceased with the matter-of-fact details of his name, parentage, length of life (the ancients were meticulous in recording this fact even to the number of days as well as years and months a person lived), and professional or social distinctions. Such a record, one would expect, would have been right and fitting for the dead girl. And since we have absolutely no evidence that women were especially reverenced as priestesses by the Etruscans, it follows that there would be no justification for wrapping the girl's body in a book of ritual.

We are forced, then, to accept the alternative theory that the linen bindings and the mummy they swathed have no relevance to each other; in other words, the dead girl was not necessarily an Etruscan at all, but that the embalmers simply enfolded her in the linen wrappings that came to hand.

LEFT A canopic jar, a special type of cinerary urn, with a crude representation of the head of the deceased. Probably 6th century B.C.

RIGHT A jug with a handle made in the shape of a backward-bending nude. Probably 7th century B.C.

84

How, then, did an Etruscan book written on linen find its way to Egypt? The answer to this question is not all that difficult. The fact that the text was not written on papyrus, which was cheaper than linen in Egypt, indicates that the linen roll was brought to Egypt by Etruscan colonists, either at the time of their initial migration from Lydia in the ninth century B.C. or at the time of their final conquest by the Romans around the first century B.C. The practice of preserving important documents on linen was certainly characteristic of the early Mediterranean peoples, for we hear of the holy books of the Samnites being recorded in this way, as well as the registers of the Roman magistrates in early Republican times.

What, then, can we learn from the Book of the Mummy?

Even though we still cannot read it, we can at least guess at its contents. It is undoubtedly a document concerned with the ritual which formed part of the famous Etruscan Discipline, or the religious code of the Etruscan people. It is known that there were twelve books describing this Discipline which laid down the methods of divination, the rules governing the relationship between men and gods, and the rituals of divine worship. The Book of the Mummy could, then, be a sacred calendar because:

1 each chapter *seems* to begin with a date;

2 there is a frequent repetition of the known word for 'god(s)' (*ais, aiser, eis, eiser*; and

3 the sound and form of the mysterious words are dithyrambic, like the responses made by a congregation to the prayer of a priest. Read this aloud:

> male ceia hia
> > etnam ciz vacl trin velthre
> male ceia hia
> > etnam ciz vacle ais vale
> male ceia hia
> > trinth etnam ciz ale
> male ceia hia
> > etnam ciz vacle vile vale

But this is about all that we know concerning the Zagreb mummy book which, if we could translate it, would not only give us the key to the Etruscan language, but would elucidate many of those mysteries which men have been trying to solve since the eighteenth-century antiquarian Giorgio Zanetti first strolled in a woodland glade in the moonlight, 'thinking deeply on the explanation of certain Etruscan letters'.

The search for the Etruscans, then, goes on, even if after hundreds of years of speculation we seem no nearer a definitive conclusion as to who they were, where they came from, and why they disappeared from the Tuscan hills as mysteriously as they arrived. Many searchers, laymen as well as scholars, have examined such facts as are available, and have advanced their theories concerning

An Etruscan bronze belt found at Bologna, the capital of northern Etruria.

them. The philologists and professional Etruscologists sooner or later base their research on the Etruscan language, for there is no doubt that the decipherment of this language would ultimately give us the key to the mystery, as the decipherment of Linear B solved the mystery of a script that was once called Minoan and proved to be Greek. Yet there are many students of the problem who admit that we shall never now break the Etruscan cipher, unless an adequate bilingual inscription comparable to the Rosetta Stone is found among the ruins of the Etruscan cities, notably those on the old frontiers between Rome and the Confederation. That such a bilingual has not been found is undoubtedly due to the haphazard way in which Etruscan archaeology was conducted until quite recently. Inscriptions meant nothing to the early treasure hunters and, in any case, there have been so many rewarding cemeteries to excavate that the patient exploration of city sites has scarcely been undertaken at all. The Etruscan

86   language, therefore, remains the almost exclusive province of the philologists,

who seem to spend an enormous amount of time and scholarship in going over and over the few scattered clues available.

All such philological problems were of no interest whatsoever to D. H. Lawrence who, by means of a long essay called *Etruscan Places*, probably did more to popularize these mysterious people than any other writer on the subject, even including George Dennis. It is not difficult to see why if one opens Lawrence's book after reading Burton's *Etruscan Bologna*. Lawrence was in the tradition of Dennis, both in his method of treating the subject and in his manner of writing about it. But Lawrence possessed a quality that no other Etruscologist had ever had before, whether British or foreign: namely, the artist's sensitivity which enabled him to reach across the ages and to see living *people* and not merely broken monuments. Not even George Dennis had been able to make the Etruscans wholly credible, however close he got to them in the ruins of their cities and cemeteries.

Lawrence, of course, was no professional Etruscologist. In fact, that was the last thing he wanted to be, for he was an inveterate enemy of the scientific approach. In *Etruscan Places* he enlivens the journey we take with him to the tombs of Tarquinia by his observations on a young German professor who is assuredly going to occupy the chair of Etruscology in some northern university, yet who displays a complete lack of interest in, let alone love for, his subject. To all Lawrence's eager questions as to what something means, as to what the dead artist is trying to say, the German replies wearily 'Nothing, nothing.' Lawrence's approach was in complete contrast. He was emotionally involved with the Etruscans who for him were not a subject for scientific analysis but a people who, like Lawrence himself, had a profound belief in life. He expresses this in his characteristic fashion in describing one of the paintings in the Tomb of the Painted Vases:

> On the end wall is a gentle little banquet scene, the bearded man softly touching the woman with him under the chin. . . . Rather gentle and lovely is the way he touches the woman under the chin, with a delicate caress that again is one of the charms of the Etruscan paintings: they really have the sense of touch; the people and the creatures are all really in touch. It is one of the rarest qualities in life as in art. There is plenty of pawing and laying hold, but no real touch. . . . Here, in this faded Etruscan painting, there is a quiet flow of touch that unites the man and woman on the couch.[1]

It can be seen at once from this passage how intuitive Lawrence's approach to the Etruscans was, especially in contrast to the rational approach of the archaeologists, philologists, and art historians. It follows from this that he was bound to be regarded as an outsider by the professors, who seldom mention *Etruscan Places* in their bibliographies. Yet Lawrence did not simply make a quick tour of Etruria in order to see the celebrated tombs and then to write a series of purple passages about life and art. He prepared himself conscientiously for his task and had, in fact, been researching the whole subject of the Etruscans since 1920 when he went to live in Italy. It is scarcely possible to live in Italy, of course, without becoming fascinated by the Etruscans, especially if, like Lawrence, one obtains the impression of a people freer, gayer, and more life-enhancing than the Romans, 'those Prussians of the ancient world'. And so Lawrence spent six or seven years sporadically studying the Etruscans through the exhibits in the museums of Rome, Florence, and Perugia, and in the writings of the specialists, particularly of George Dennis who was a man after the novelist's own heart. In fact, when Lawrence eventually set off on his journeys to the Etruscan sites in 1927, he undoubtedly had *Cities and Cemeteries* in his knapsack and, for that matter, his debt to this book is obvious. Moreover, the debt is not only that of borrowing Dennis's facts but also of using his methods. Dennis always leads us to the Etruscan sites by way of the living towns and people he met on the road and he always puts us in a good humour by describing his host or hostess or guide. Lawrence intuitively recognized the merits of this

A primitive Etruscan statuette of Menrva or Minerva, the Etruscan warrior-goddess who corresponded to the Greeks' Athene. She belonged to the trinity comprised of Tinia (Jupiter), Uni (Juno), and Menrva.

[1] D. H. Lawrence, *Etruscan Places* (Harmondsworth: Penguin Books, 1950), pp. 73–4.

approach to a difficult subject like the Etruscans, whom he particularly wanted to free from the smell of the lamp and to present to his readers as human beings, not the 'mystery people of the ancient world'. To do so he, like Dennis, takes us on a journey which begins in the present and leads us easily into the past. George Dennis, writing about his arrival in Tarquinia in 1843, first introduces us to Carlo Avvolta, the doyen of the early Etruscan excavators, and describes him in this manner:

> The visitor to Corneto (the old name of Tarquinia) will do well to obtain an intro/duction to Signor Carlo Avvolta, once the *gonfaloniere*, or chief magistrate of the city, now a *consultore*, or counsellor of Civita Vecchia. He is a lively, intelligent old gentle/man, experienced in excavations, deeply interested in the antiquities of this site, his birthplace, ever ready to impart information and displaying as much courtesy to strangers as cordiality to his friends. Such as feel little interest in antiquities may consult him with profit on the more rousing matters of Maremma sports. Though now nearly eighty years of age, he is still a keen sportsman and enters on the fatigues and perils of the chase with the ardour of a man of thirty. He resides in a spacious, gloomy house, where everything breathes of antiquity; but wherever his activity may lead him during the day, in the evening he is sure to be found in the *caffe*, or at the *spezieria*, where he will descant, with all the enthusiasm of his nature, on the last boar or roe/buck he made to bite the dust, or on the paintings and furniture of Etruscan tombs.[1]

Eighty-four years later, Lawrence arrived in Tarquinia and found the place itself scarcely changed since Dennis had passed that way, though today it would be almost unrecognizable to either man. And like his predecessor, Lawrence makes us feel that we are not merely spectators but companions on his travels. We go with Dennis to the *caffe* to meet his lively old gentleman; and with Lawrence to meet a boy:

> A little lad in long trousers who would seem to be only twelve years old but who has the air of a mature man, confronts us with his chest out. We ask for rooms. He eyes us, darts away for the key, and leads us off upstairs another flight, shouting to a young girl who acts as chambermaid, to follow on. . . . He was, in fact, the most manly and fatherly little hotel manager I have ever known, and he ran the whole place. He was in reality fourteen years old, but stunted. From five in the morning till ten at night he was on the go, never ceasing, and with a queer, abrupt, sideways/darting alacrity that must have wasted a great deal of energy. The father and mother were in the background – quite young and pleasant. But they didn't seem to exert themselves. Albertino did it all.[2]

Despite his years of study and his special tour of the Etruscan places (though only four of them – Cerveteri, Tarquinia, Vulci, and Volterra), Lawrence did not consider the Etruscans or their works as an academic subject about which he was commissioned to write a history. He uses them as a peg on which to hang his own ideas, indeed, his own life view, which was very different from that of the conventional scholar. And it is this which makes his book so valuable, for he was the first writer after Dennis to treat the Etruscans as a living and not an

An ivory statuette of a goddess, 675–650 B.C., originally covered in gold leaf. It was found at Marsiliana d'Albegna, the site of a lost Etruscan city.

[1] George Dennis, *Cities and Cemeteries of Etruria* (London: Dent, Everyman's Library, 1907), vol. I, p. 318.
[2] Lawrence, *op. cit.*, p. 45.

extinct people. And more than that, Lawrence, an artist himself, first drew the world's attention to the special qualities of Etruscan art – the freshness and gaiety of their paintings, the liveliness and humour of their sculptures. Speaking of the urns in the museum at Volterra, Professor Pericle Ducati says, characteristically, that while their artistic interest is small, they are valuable for the mythological scenes they portray. Nonsense, says Lawrence. By 'artistic' the academicians always mean Greek; and that is why Etruscan artefacts have never been thought of as other than museum exhibits. The mythological scenes – Helen and the Dioscuri, Medea fleeing from Corinth, Oedipus and the Sphinx – are just so many Greek subjects which no longer have any particular meaning for us, whereas the Etruscan artists' depiction of scenes from actual life – departures in covered wagons, ships sailing away, girls reading open scrolls – suddenly reveal to us living Etruscans as the contemporary artists saw them, without the restraints of Greek artistic conventions.

And so Lawrence remained eloquently anti-museum in his appraisal of the Etruscans and sums up his view in this famous passage:

> The Florence Museum is vastly instructive, if you want object lessons about the Etruscans. But who wants object lessons about vanished races? What one wants is contact. The Etruscans are not a theory or a thesis. If they are anything, they are an *experience*.
>
> And the experience is always spoilt. Museums, museums, museums, object lessons rigged out to illustrate the unsound theories of archaeologists, crazy attempts to coordinate and get into a fixed order that which has no fixed order and will not be coordinated. It is sickening! Why must all experience be systematized? Why must even the vanished Etruscans be reduced to a system? They never will be.[1]

A 19th-century drawing of the Etruscan Museum at Florence. This Museum still contains the famous bronze statue 'The Orator' seen here from the back.

[1] Lawrence, *op. cit.*, p. 167.

Wherever he discusses things Etruscan, whether it is their tomb paintings or their bronzes or their burial urns, Lawrence always allows his feelings as an artist and a lover of freedom to interpret what he sees: in other words, he uses his senses and not his intellect. The result, of course, is a highly personal view of the Etruscans – the view, in fact, of an exiled Englishman, a novelist of genius, and one of the most original thinkers of his time. And it is quite possible that he may be all wrong in his conclusions. Indeed, from the point of view of many historians his analysis of Etruscan society, based as it is on a great deal of personal emotion and very little factual evidence, is superficial and misleading. The Etruscans' obsession with death, their sinister network of underground tombs, their religion of hopelessness and fear, and their cruel treatment of prisoners of war, it could be argued, tell the rational observer a very different story from the pictures of the dancers, musicians, and loving couples reclining at the banquet table. Certainly Lawrence could have deluded himself and could be deluding us by reason of his life-enhancing views and his supreme art of expressing those views. And so even though he did liberate us, as it were, from the didacticism of the schools and showed the way for us to draw our own conclusions as to the culture, philosophy, art, and religion of the Etruscans, we should balance the Lawrentian flights of fancy with the facts painstakingly collected for us by lesser writers but better scholars like Thomas Dempster and George Dennis and many others whose works also deserve to be remembered.

The François vase, found near Chiusi in 1844. The Athenian painter, Kleitias, has included nearly two-hundred figures in his design. The mythological subjects illustrated include the return of Theseus after his victory over the Minotaur, the hunt for the Kalydon boar, and the chariot races at the funeral of Patroclus.

CHAPTER SIX

The American Pioneers

I T WAS HARDLY to be expected that the Etruscans would be of much interest in the mid-nineteenth century to Americans who were in the process of discovering and developing their own continent. But at the same time, this was an age in the United States, as in Europe, of enormous intellectual curiosity, distinguished perhaps more than any other period in history by the enterprise of brilliant explorers and travellers. American members of this band of brave and gifted pioneers were already wandering about the un-mapped regions of Africa, Asia, and the Middle East, sometimes crossing the paths of the European explorers.

Charles Godfrey Leland was one such American explorer. He was born in Philadelphia in 1824 and died in Florence, Italy, in 1903. One sees from the place of his death that he was something of an exile, though his body was taken home to be buried in Laurel Hill Cemetery in Philadelphia. But in those days many American adventurers lived abroad not because they wished to expatriate themselves, but because they regarded themselves as citizens of the world; and nobody exemplified this attitude more than C. G. Leland.

If we look at the Library of Congress *Catalog of Printed Cards*, we find almost four pages of close print devoted to this author's productions, from one of the first entries, *The alternate sex; or, The female intellect in man and the masculine in woman*, published in New York in 1904; to the last, *Wood carving . . . 5th edition* (reprinted), London, New York, 1931. In between there are seventy-three titles to choose from, many of them, however, reprints of his more popular works like the *Hans Breitmann Ballads* and his numerous books on gypsies.

But then consider the titles of some of his other productions:

The art of conversation, with directions for self-education (1874)

Comment cultiver la Volonté (1911)

Dyes, stains, inks, lacquers, varnishes and polishes (1899)

Elementary metal work (1900)

The English Gypsies and their language (1873)

Algonkin poems, translated metrically (1902)

Fusang; or, The discovery of America by Chinese Buddhist priests in the fifth century (1895)

Leather work. A practical manual for learners (1892) and, concerning us,

Etruscan Roman remains in popular tradition (1892)

Charles Godfrey Leland (1824–1903), an American Etruscologist and specialist on English gypsies.

Fresco from a 4th-century B.C. tomb discovered at Orvieto, depicting the deceased departing in his chariot for the Underworld.

How, we ask, did one man have enough time and knowledge to write about a fifth-century Chinese navigator, methods of leather and metal work, the poetry of the Algonkin Indians, the language of the English gypsies (including the discovery of an ancient Romany dialect called Shelta), and the mythology of the Etruscans? Does Leland himself supply the answer to our instinctive doubts in his introduction to *Etruscan Roman remains*?

> As it indeed befell me myself once in Bath, where it was declared in a large gypsy encampment that I must be either Romany or of Romany blood, because I was the biggest liar they had ever met.[1]

But the answer is not that simple, and Leland does not stand self-condemned. Far from being a liar or sensationalist he was a genuine scholar, a good linguist, a brilliant ethnologist, and an accomplished craftsman in wood, leather, and metal working. This range and variety of skills was not, in fact, untypical of the class of men to which he belonged. Nineteenth-century exploration, in fact, was made possible largely by the resourcefulness of such amateur polymaths. And Leland had other attributes which were also characteristic of his time: he was an exuberant and humorous man who did not see why knowledge should make him solemn. In this he resembled his famous English contemporaries Henry Layard, George Dennis, and Sir Richard Burton, all three of whom were

[1] Charles Godfrey Leland, *Etruscan Roman remains in popular tradition* (London: T. Fisher Unwin, 1892), p. 3.

sceptical of the orthodox piety of their age and tolerant of human weaknesses. Leland's attitudes to life appeared early in his education, for we find him at the College of New Jersey rebelling against the sanctimoniousness of the régime. It was probably official piety and his own unorthodox views which prompted him to go abroad to the universities of Heidelberg and Munich where, it is said, 'he developed into a burly, genial giant of a man, with a beard like Charlemagne's and a gargantuan appetite for food, drink, and tobacco'. The description tells us a great deal that we need to know about this splendid American adventurer, who fought as a captain in the revolutionary army on the Paris barricades in 1848.

At twenty-five, Leland was a typical mid-nineteenth-century wanderer: in addition to the thorough classical education then in vogue even at American universities, he had studied German literature and life at Heidelberg and French literature and public affairs at the Sorbonne. He was the kind of scholar who could translate Heine, write a book of popular psychology in French (*Comment cultiver la Volonté*), and study at first hand such diverse languages as Algonquian Indian, Celtic, and Romany. All of his considerable intellectual attainments, moreover, were combined with a life of continuous travel and adventure. His decision to fight with the French revolutionaries on the barricades of Paris in 1848 is typical. It was inevitable, too, that he should return home in order to enlist in a Philadelphia artillery company in 1863 and to be present at the Battle of Gettysburg.

During his years in America, from 1849 to 1869, after which date he moved to London, Leland was actively engaged in contemporary American journalism, which should not be confused with newspaper reporting as it exists today. Journalism in the mid-nineteenth century, in every country of the civilized world, was as definite a branch of literature as fiction, poetry, or the essay. It was, in fact, still practised in the tradition of literary artists like Addison, Dr Johnson, Defoe, Hazlitt, and Dickens in England; Benjamin Franklin, Mark Twain, and Theodore Roosevelt in America. Even the popular journals and magazines were written and edited on the assumption that their readership was intelligent, literate, and, above all, anxious to improve their minds. The concept of 'mass media' by which the sum of individuals is equated with a faceless and mindless populace was not the main determinant of nineteenth-century journalism. Consequently, a writer like Charles Leland could submit essays on art, German poetry, and classical themes to a whole variety of popular magazines and newspapers, and actually earn his living by doing so.

In 1869, he set off again for Europe, and spent several years wandering about with the British gypsies, on whom he became an authority, writing several definitive books on this people. *The English Gypsies and their language*, published in 1873, is still a classic of the subject. And as if his researches into the customs and dialects of the gypsies were not enough, he devoted himself to a study of the industrial arts and wrote a series of textbooks on metal and leather work,

Head of a woman. Many such heads in clay, terracotta, or bronze were placed on the lids of cinerary urns, all showing the influence of Greek models but revealing at the same time the innate taste of the Etruscan artists.

94

printing, engraving, and inks. He was now interested in reforming elementary education in his own country, and so returned in 1879 to America to promote his policies and schemes in the schools of the eastern states. When this task was completed, he turned his attention to something entirely different; and in this he showed himself a product of his time and place, for the late nineteenth century in the United States was a period of obsessive interest in the occult, manifested in the popularity of many pseudo-mystical cults like spiritualism, Rosicrucianism, theosophy, astrology, and the like. Leland, however, was too hard-headed to identify himself with any particular movement, and his interest in the occult remained that of an inquirer. But from then on, he became a fervent student of magic as it is found in the old myths and legends of unsophisticated peoples. It was this interest in legends, and particularly in witchcraft, which finally took him to Italy in search of the lost Etruscan religious beliefs.

His book *Etruscan Roman remains in popular tradition*, the result of many years of study and research, is now out of print and unread, but it remains a valuable, indeed an invaluable, record of a world that has almost disappeared: namely, the world of pre-industrial, rural Italy in the 1890s. Leland describes the last vestiges of the paganism of the old Mediterranean and Etruscan worlds before either the Roman or the Christian ethos replaced the ancient animism with their entirely new concepts. He tells us that witchcraft, which he rightly identifies with *la vecchia religione* (the old religion), was far more prevalent than even the Italians of the big cities realized; and he proves his point by reporting the legends, spells, and magical cures which he learned about during his sojourn among the Tuscan peasants. He argues on the basis of his extensive experience with gypsies, tinkers, and tramps, that the possessors of this ancient lore, 'certain cryptic witches and a few obscure wizards who belong to mystic families', were fearful of priests, cultured people, and 'all the powers that be', just as gypsies and tramps distrust everyone who is not 'on the road', or all honest folk. It is a shrewd observation which explains why professional anthropologists and armchair mythologists may be so far from the truth in their interpretations. If, on the other hand, we accept Leland's contention as true, then it might well be asked how a well-to-do American visitor managed to gain the confidence of 'certain cryptic witches and a few obscure wizards'; and if he did not, or could not gain that confidence, are his accounts of myths, incantations, and magical cures reliable?

The answer seems to be that Leland was, as we know from contemporary accounts, a very congenial person and, being an American, much less class conscious than the average European of the time; and these two qualities of congeniality and absence of social prejudice appear to have enabled him to communicate easily and naturally with all those people outside the confines of polite society – the people 'on the road' in Britain, the dispossessed Indians of New England, and the *contadini* of Tuscan Romagna. Or, as he puts it: 'As chief of the English gypsies – or at least as President of the English Gypsy-Lore Society,

The Judgment of Paris. Decoration on a late 4th-century B.C. cista, probably a cylindrical container for cosmetics. This famous beauty contest was a favourite legend with the Etruscans.

which amounts to the same thing – I have a natural proclivity for ways that are dark and low society. . . .' In Tuscany, his informants were principally old women whose confidence he managed to obtain by his open and friendly approach and, no doubt, many small gifts; for he tells us that he 'was not un-generous of pounds of coffee, small bottles of rum, cigars, and other minor requisites which greatly promote conviviality and mutual understanding in wisdom'. But his chief advantage lay in the fact that he was obviously not a representative of, or spy for, authority, either ecclesiastical or civil. For the 'witches' he consulted were, like peasants everywhere in Italy, suspicious of the local priests and police, and even while publicly claiming to be good Catholics – and wearing a medal to prove it – secretly held to the beliefs, myths, cures, and spells of their pagan ancestors – *la vecchia religione*. Leland himself admits that his task in finding out their secrets was extremely difficult; and there is no doubt that he was fed a great deal of mumbo-jumbo by canny peasants among whom the news was undoubtedly circulated that a rich American was paying good money for fancy talk. But he points out quite legitimately that the illiterate old women who were his principal informants could no more have invented the little prayers to Pan and Bacchus which he records than they could have invented the flying machine, inasmuch as these poems have woven into them the most classical allusions and characteristics.

What is certain from all this is that Leland has demonstrated that some of the old Etruscan gods survived in their names, attributes, and appeal up to the end of the nineteenth century, a life span of almost three thousand years. In fact, one could conclude that this paganism, which was certainly a living cult throughout medieval Europe, was finally destroyed in its last strongholds not by the Church, or even by popular education, but by industrialization and mechanization. The spirits which pagans, ancient or modern, believe inhabit every living thing, plant, or animal, cannot, it seems, survive the noise and pollution of modern machines any more than large tracts of forest and field can survive them. And so it would be true to say that Leland's researches are, in a sense, archaic; and one very much doubts whether there is an old woman left in all Tuscany who could recite the Spell of the Spider, the Green Lizard, or the Falling Star, which the American anthropologist has recorded for us.

But the student of Etruscology trying to penetrate the mystery of the Etruscan pantheon should be grateful to Leland's devoted work to the extent that his researches prove the vitality of the old religion, which was the religion of the Mediterranean world *before* the Greeks and Romans civilized society into the form which we have inherited from them. He proves, too, that gods like Aplu (the Greek Apollo), Fufluns (Dionysus), and Turan (Aphrodite) were both real and personal to their devotees, perhaps much more than the gods who supplanted them were to later generations. Thus, the Etruscan Aplu actually retained both his name and his attributes in the villages of Etruria where he was

The frontispiece to Leland's *Gypsy Sorcery*. Leland also investigated Etruscan magic as it survived in the Tuscan countryside.

still 'the most beautiful of all male spirits' and where he still had his own hymn which Leland gives as follows:

> Aplu, Aplu, Aplu!
> Tu che sei buono, tanto di sapienza!
> E sei dotto e di talento,
> Aplu, Aplu, Aplu!
> Io ti prego darmi
> Fortuna e talento.

In English:

> Aplu, Aplu, Aplu!
> Thou who art so good and wise,
> So learned and so talented,
> Aplu, Aplu, Aplu!
> I pray thee give me
> Fortune and talent.[1]

The Etruscan goddess Turan survives as the good fairy Turanna, the spirit of peace and love. She, too, has her hymns of praise. Fufluns, the origin of whose Etruscan name is a mystery, was very much alive in the vineyards of Tuscany, though now under the name of Faflon; and, according to Leland, he is the

[1] Leland, *op. cit.*, pp. 37–8.

ABOVE LEFT George Hempl (1850–1921), Professor of Philology at Stanford University and a student of the Etruscan language. RIGHT Daniel Garrison Brinton (1837–99), American physician, ethnologist, and armchair archaeologist. He tried to relate the Etruscan language to the Berber languages of North Africa.

OPPOSITE LEFT Figures from an Etruscan mirror, discussed by Charles Leland in his *Etruscan Roman remains in popular tradition.* RIGHT An Etruscan amulet in bronze against the evil eye. It was owned by Charles Leland.

subject of 'the last truly Bacchanalian song which will ever be heard on earth':

Faflon, Faflon, Faflon!
A vuoi mi raccomando!
Che l'uve nella mia vigna
E molta scarsa,
A vuoi mi raccomando,
Che mi fate avere
Buona vendemmia!

Faflon, Faflon, Faflon!
Oh listen to my prayer!
I have a poor vintage
My vines this year are bare.
Oh listen to my prayer!
And put, since thou canst do so,
A better vintage there![1]

Certainly Leland's *Etruscan Roman remains* is, like Dennis's *Cities and Cemeteries*, a classic of its kind, even though both books are no longer available, Leland's volume being obtainable only in the national libraries. But again, like Dennis, the American explorer of Etruria has that gentle humour and love of the country people and largeness of mind which he and his famous contemporaries took with them to the unexplored regions of the world, where they so often died along the road, some in Africa, some in Asia Minor, and nearly all of them far from home. But for Charles Godfrey Leland, the whole world was his home; and perhaps he sums up his own view of that world in his advice to the readers of *Etruscan Roman remains*:

I propose my book to be a guide to be followed by other and more learned or better qualified scholars and seekers. . . . And a nice time they will have of it if they walk the ways which I have walked, in the paths which I have trod.[2]

Charles Leland's compatriot, Daniel Garrison Brinton, was the American scholar of the period whose special interest was the mythology and language of

[1] Leland, *op. cit.,* p. 43.
[2] Leland, *op. cit.,* p. 2.

101

primitive peoples, among whom he included the Etruscans. But the approach of the two men to the problem was very different, as one would expect of two contemporaries whose character and attitudes were so dissimilar. Yet Charles Leland and Daniel Brinton were of roughly the same age and even of the same state, both having been born in Pennsylvania, the former in 1824; the latter in 1837. Both went to northern universities; both were good students; both showed a special aptitude for languages. A final point of resemblance is the enormous industry of the pair, for if Leland's publications cover four pages of close print in the Library of Congress *Catalog of Printed Cards*, Brinton's writings cover six pages. Again one wonders *how* these nineteenth-century researchers found the time and energy to do a regular job, travel extensively, write scores of books and hundreds of articles, and get married. Perhaps it is significant that most of them had few, if any, progeny.

But Brinton differed most fundamentally from men like Leland, Dennis, and Layard in that he was an armchair ethnologist, seldom going out into the field himself, but using (and acknowledging) the work of those who did. Again, ethnology was at first a hobby with him, arising out of his medical studies, for he graduated from the Jefferson Medical College with the degree of M.D. and practised medicine first in West Chester, Pennsylvania, and later with the Second Division of the 11th Corps of the Federal Army. Along with Charles Leland he was present at the Battle of Gettysburg, in his capacity as Surgeon-in-Chief. After the war he settled in Philadelphia, choosing to edit various medical journals and encyclopedias rather than to practise medicine.

In 1887, at the age of fifty, Brinton was able to withdraw from medicine altogether and to devote all his time to ethnology and archaeology. During the years 1887 to 1896, as Professor Emeritus at the University of Pennsylvania, he wrote a continuous stream of books and articles with titles like these:

> *The Annals of the Cakchiquels.* The Original Text, with a translation, notes and introduction by D. G. Brinton
>
> *Rig Veda Americanus. Sacred Songs of the Ancient Mexicans* . . . Edited with a paraphrase . . . by D. G. Brinton
>
> *Grammar of the Choctaw Language* . . . Edited by . . . D. G. Brinton
>
> 'Further Notes on Fuegian Languages'
>
> 'Left-handedness in North American Aboriginal Art'.

Since the quantity of academic output as well as the quality has always impressed the lay world, Dr Brinton was soon regarded as an authority not only on the American Indians, whom he made his special study, but also on distant peoples whom he had never even seen, since he obviously disliked leaving his desk. Included in the people and languages he wrote extensively upon were the Mayas and Aztecs, the Letts and Berbers, and – eventually – the Etruscans. While it is evident that this studious and industrious man was certainly not an imposter, it is equally evident that his method of research and his creed of

A portrait of Charun, the Etruscan god of the Underworld. He is armed with a hammer in order to crush his victims.

'publish or perish' resulted in more anthropological and linguistic misinformation than any other single pedant of his generation has managed to disseminate. He denied, for instance, the Mongolian origin of the American Indians and states categorically that they were of European (Aryan) derivation. He dismissed the Toltecs, or the reed people, who ruled an empire in Central Mexico between the tenth and twelfth centuries A.D., as legendary, whereas a visit to Yucatan would have shown him the many gigantic monuments which Quetzalcoatl, the Feathered Serpent, built to commemorate his god and himself. He translated the Aztec picture language by guesswork, which was admittedly customary with American amateur ethnologists of the period; and then, turning his attention to Etruscan, somehow got it into his head that this language was related to the speech of the Berbers, Kabyles, and Tuareg. He attempted to justify this hypothetical relationship in several readings he gave before the American Philosophical Society of Philadelphia. His lectures were published in the *Proceedings* of the Society under the titles 'The Ethnologic Affinities of the Ancient Etruscans,' 'On Etruscan and Libyan Names,' and 'The EtruscoLibyan Elements in the Song of the Arval Brethren.'[1] The impression one gets from these highsounding articles is that the Professor is trying to blind his lay readers with science; but the professional philologists were not at all impressed. On the contrary, they found both his linguistic and ethnological arguments faintly ridiculous; and indeed his theories as to the origin of the Etruscans and their language have been ignored or discarded.

Daniel Brinton was followed by George Hempl (1850–1921), an American of German extraction, who was a Professor of Philology at Stanford University. By the time Hempl turned his attention to the Etruscans, however, interest in the subject, which had been fairly high when Charles Leland and Daniel Brinton were writing, had waned. Etruscology was now an academic discipline of scant interest to American historians, ethnologists, or, for that matter, the general public. Hence Hempl's attempts to prove that Etruscan and Latin were sister languages and in their early state indistinguishable the one from the other was ignored at home and regarded with scepticism abroad.

Recent American scholars who have been at all interested in Etruscology have avoided the dangers which the subject so obviously presents and have conformed to the current academic philosophy and methodology of never deviating from the orthodox line. We shall probably never see another Charles Leland and can hardly expect to in view of the disappearance of the Etruria which he knew. Nor of course do modern scholars take the risks incurred by Daniel Brinton in identifying an unknown with a known language and then, with the aid of a good imagination, translating it into English. The competition in the academies is far too severe to permit a professor to commit himself like that. In consequence, perhaps the best way to know the Etruscans is to leave the studies and the books behind and to go back to the places where they lived.

A family tomb at Volterra, reconstructed in the grounds of the Archaeological Museum, Florence. The deceased are shown reclining on their sarcophagi as though still gazing at the passing world.

[1] D. G. Brinton, *Proceedings of the American Philosophical Society* (Philadelphia), vols. XXVI (1864), XXVIII (1866), and XXX (1868).

Part Two
The Discoveries

CHAPTER SEVEN

The City-States

GEORGE DENNIS was undoubtedly over-optimistic in claiming that we can now 'enter into the inner life of the Etruscans almost as fully as if they were living and moving before us, instead of having been extinct as a nation for more than two thousand years'.[1] Despite the quantity of new evidence accumulated since 1847 when he made this statement, the Etruscologist today would be inclined to take almost the opposite view; namely, that the mystery of the Etruscan civilization, and in particular the obscurity surrounding its inner life, is profounder than ever.

Why should this be so? The answer is that our failure to find the key to the Etruscan language means that the door to this inner life – to the private thoughts of the ordinary citizen – remains closed to us, just as it did, for instance, in the case of the Babylonians until we were able to read the law code of Hammurabi, a social document which suddenly revealed such aspects of ancient Meso-potamian life as the rights of women, the place of a wife in the home, the status of the different classes of citizens, and the nature of crime and punishment. Without this document and other social and literary texts left us in the library of King Ashurbanipal, the story of the Babylonians could only be told in the form of the surviving monuments and the statues of unidentifiable monarchs; and neither monuments nor statues can throw much light on the inner life of the ordinary people.

We suffer because many other nations of the ancient world have the same inability to speak to us directly, even peoples as civilized as the Phoenicians and Carthaginians, those master mariners of the pre-Columbian Age. It is true that we can read and understand the few Punic records – mostly funerary inscriptions – that have survived; but what a different view we would have of the world, African as well as north European, if the libraries of Carthage had not been destroyed along with the rest of that city! Instead we can only learn about Phoenicians, Carthaginians, and Etruscans from their inveterate enemies, the Greeks and Romans. They cannot speak for themselves or defend their life view or justify their conduct and so elicit our sympathy or admiration.

On the other hand, the sheer quantity of their artefacts enables us to catch at least a glimpse of certain aspects of Etruscan life, though chiefly of the ruling class which could afford to commemorate itself in monuments. These artefacts

[1] George Dennis, *Cities and Cemeteries of Etruria* (London: Dent, Everyman's Library, 1907), vol. I, p. 2.

Detail from a painting
in the Tomb of Golini
at Orvieto, depicting a
servant preparing vessels
for a banquet.

show us, for instance, what an Etruscan nobleman and his spouse looked like, because we have a number of sarcophagi with effigies of the deceased marital pair upon the lids. We can even tell from these statues and from paintings in the tombs what costume, headgear, and ornaments a well-dressed citizen and his wife wore. But we cannot tell from looking at their likenesses in stone what these people thought and did in their day-to-day lives, what the insides of their houses were like, what were their favourite foods, what they read, what their children learned in school, and all those minor *human* activities which we can reconstruct from the literature of the Greeks and Romans, and even of the Egyptians and Babylonians. Moreover, the Greek and Roman authors who knew the Etruscans at first hand tell us so little about them that the two historians who actually came from the same region as the Etruscans – Herodotus and Dionysius, both of Halicarnassus in Caria (today south-western Turkey) – disagree as to the provenance of this mysterious people. Herodotus definitely states that they migrated to Italy from Lydia. Dionysius as definitely argues that they did not, but were indigenous to Italy. Yet both writers had access to the same sources, notably the *History of Lydia*, written by one Xanthus, a native of that country. Such is the confusion concerning the origin and history of one of the great nations of the ancient world.

But regardless of where the Etruscans originally came from, we know that they were established on the Tuscan hills by the eighth century B.C., at a period when the Greeks were first setting up trading posts on the east coast of Sicily. 107

Indeed, the fleets of the two nations were already beginning to clash, whence arose the Greek accusation of 'piratical Tyrrhenians'. What this term actually signifies is that the Etruscans had naval supremacy in the western Mediterranean from a very early period, from the beginning of the Iron Age, in fact. Such command of the sea by one nation was – from the beginning of recorded history up to the end of the eighteenth century – invariably called piracy by rival maritime powers.

The sea battles between Greeks and Etruscans, Greeks and Carthaginians, Carthaginians and Etruscans were, of course, fought for control of the trade routes, for with the coming of the Iron Age the mines of Elba, Sardinia, and Etruria provided the lifeblood of the Mediterranean empires. As long as the Etruscans ruled the seas around the western shores of Italy, therefore, they could exact what tribute they liked to allow the iron, copper, gold, and silver of the mines to be exported to the Greek and Egyptian manufactories. The evidence of the wealth they thus acquired is demonstrated by the thousands of imported ready-made goods which have been found in their tombs, proving that the merchant ships carried cargoes of vases, ornaments, and various manufactured articles to Etruria in return for raw materials, particularly the iron needed to equip the armies of Persia and Greece. Once Etruria lost control of the seas to the Carthaginians, however, her role as an international force began to decline. She now turned her attention to internal territorial conquests and began the absorption of large areas of Italy into her empire.

At that time – namely the seventh and sixth centuries B.C. – Italy was a country of diverse tribes, as in fact was the whole of Europe outside the eastern Mediterranean. These tribes, Italic, Gallic, Germanic, or British, were still living in the early Iron Age: their social system was based on the clan whose chieftain was at once a king, a high priest, and a father figure. They lived in village settlements – sometimes on lakes – and supplied their needs by primitive agriculture, cattle raising, and fishing. In the Italian peninsula there were a dozen tribes or more, of whom the principal clans were the Ligurians in the north-west, the Veneti in the north-east, the Umbrians and the Samnites in the centre, the Latins in the west, and various groups in the foot of the peninsula, which was to become the region of Greek colonization, or Magna Greca. The Etruscans, once they were firmly established in Tuscany, were greatly superior militarily as well as culturally to their neighbours and hence had no great difficulty in imposing their dominion on these various Italic tribes. They penetrated far to the north and to the south of their original homeland, though whether in organized wars of conquest or as 'trade missions' we have no way of telling.

One concludes, in the absence of any of their own histories, that the Etruscans were not as martial a nation as the Greeks under Alexander of Macedon, or the Carthaginians under Hannibal, or the Romans under Sulla. On the other

The Ficoroni Cista, the largest and most beautiful of the containers found at Palestrina. The handle is made up of the figure of Dionysius supported by two satyrs. Details of the engravings on the sides appear overleaf.

hand, it is difficult to estimate their military prowess in view of the contradictions as well as the scantiness of the evidence, particularly since our principal sources of information are the Roman historians who were writing at a period when Etruria no longer existed as an independent nation, but had become a colony of Rome. Yet the Etruscan kings and heroes were still remembered as the mortal foes of the Roman people in the historians' accounts of the old wars. Livy, for instance, as the self-appointed apologist of the Augustan Age, finds very little good to say of the defeated enemy, particularly in view of his need to flatter Augustus and to justify the new imperialism. We cannot, therefore, be sure of the accuracy of Livy's account, though he does provide us with a clue to the reason for the collapse of the Etruscan Confederation. He tells us, for instance, that the Etruscan military policy was based on the prosecution of private wars for gain: in other words, they used organized plundering expeditions of armed bands led by warrior princes. But when it came to the defence of the homeland on a national scale, the leaders were obliged to employ mercenaries, even including their old enemies the Gauls, a practice which was typical of all oriental or orientalized states from the time of Babylon. The Carthaginians, too, had relied on mercenaries, whereas the Romans, at least in the good old days of the Republic, had allowed none but citizens to serve in their legions. The Etruscans and the Carthaginians paid dearly for their belief that they could buy their national security by arming mercenaries and slaves; for in the case of the former people, during the great emergency of 308 B.C. when the last decisive battle was fought between the Etruscans and Romans at Lake Vadimon about forty miles north of the capital, the Romans had a well-trained and disciplined citizens' army, while the Etruscans relied on each recruit

Scenes of the voyage of the Argonauts from the Ficoroni Cista: ABOVE Pollux, after defeating Amico in a boxing match, ties him to a tree, and OPPOSITE Argonauts in their ship *Argo* which was built under the supervision of Athena.

naming another man for enlistment, the second man naming a third, and so on. With this hodge-podge of unwilling conscripts and any mercenaries they could hire, the Etruscans joined battle with their old enemies at Vadimon. The result was complete defeat – so much so, says Livy, that 'on this day, for the first time, the power of the Etruscans was broken. The main part of their troops fell in battle; their camp was taken by storm and plundered.'[1]

If, then, the Etruscan army was raised in such a haphazard manner and consisted largely of serfs forced to fight because some friend – or more likely some enemy – had named them, it is difficult to see how they could have withstood an army of free and responsible citizens like the Romans who began to take the field against Veii, their ancient rival. Yet in the heyday of Etruscan power their conquests included not only vast areas of the mainland, but outposts on various offshore islands like Elba, Corsica, and possibly Sardinia. They probably gained possession of these territories partly by armed incursions, then by trade missions, and finally by the imposition of their superior culture on the backward nations whose leaders quickly accepted the amenities of civilized living.

One fact is clear in this early history of Etruscan conquest: these people never formed one unified nation with a single national policy, but belonged to at least twelve separate states, each state represented by a capital city, precisely as Greece was a nation of city-states or, for that matter, as Italy remained throughout the Middle Ages. Under this loose federation, a united front was, for the most part, a matter of expediency, a fact which was to lead to the eventual downfall of Etruria as an independent nation. And by the same token, the absence of concerted action on the military front meant both a practical and a psychological

Titus Livius, *Ab Urbe Condita*, IX, 39.

weakness in times of peace as well as of war. In short, the Twelve were rivals and allies at one and the same time, and defeat was inevitable when they ceased to be allies.

This type of federation between city-states whose citizens spoke a common language and belonged to the same culture, far from being uncommon in the pre-Roman world, was the normal socio-political system, since ancient peoples, newly emerged from tribalism, did not think, as we do, in terms of nations and empires, but of their village and of their immediate kith and kin. The ordinary citizen owed his allegiance to the clan chieftain who, as his dominions increased in extent, called himself a king or, as the Greeks termed him, a tyrant. So the individual Etruscan belonged not to a nation called Etruria, but to one or another of its city-states. Yet so inconclusive is our knowledge that there is no certainty as to which cities these Twelve were; even those writers nearest them in time do not agree in naming them. The fact is that there were many more than twelve principal cities since the country occupied by the Etruscans, or eventually colonized by them, was divided into provinces: Southern Etruria, sometimes referred to as Etruria Proper, which included cities like Veii, Caere, Tarquinii, and Sutrium; and Northern Etruria, comprising the modern province of Emilia-Romagna and including Rusellae, Vetulonia, Clusium, Volaterrae, and a dozen others. There were also Etruscan settlements north of the Apennines at Mantua, Modena, Parma, and Piacenza. Consequently authors, ancient and modern, are confused as to which were the undisputed Twelve Cities of the Etruscan league, which is understandable since the fame and fortunes of the individual towns rose and fell during the seven centuries of the Etruscan *imperium*. However, a working list based on the testimony of classical authors is as follows:

Ancient name	Modern name
Tarquinii	Tarquinia
Caere	Cerveteri
Vulci	Ponte della Badia
Rusellae	Roselle
Vetulonia	Poggio Colonna (?)
Populonia	Porto Baratti
Volsinii	Bolsena
Clusium	Chiusi
Arretium	Arezzo
Perusia	Perugia
Volaterrae	Volterra
Faesulae	Fiesole
or Cortona (?)	Cortona

In addition to these twelve famous cities whose names and sites were never altogether lost, there were hundreds of other Etruscan cities, townships, and

Map of Etruria, with an inset showing its location on the Italian peninsula.

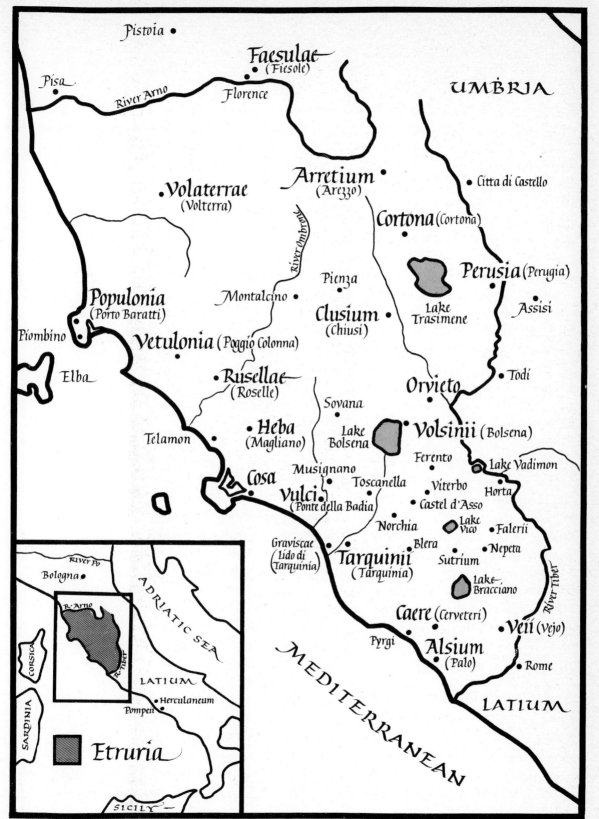

Pistoia •

Faesulae
(Fiesole) •

Pisa •

UMBRIA

River Arno

Florence •

Volaterrae
(Volterra) •

Arretium
(Arezzo)

Citta di Castello •

River Ombrone

Cortona (Cortona) •

Perusia (Perugia) •

Pienza •

Lake
Trasimene

Assisi •

Populonia
(Porto Baratti) •

Montalcino •

Clusium
(Chiusi) •

Piombino

Vetulonia (Poggio Colonna) •

Elba

Rusellae
(Roselle) •

Sovana •

Orvieto •

Todi •

Heba
(Magliano) •

Lake
Bolsena

Volsinii (Bolsena) •

Telamon •

Ferento •

Lake Vadimon

Musignano •

Cosa

Toscanella •

Viterbo •

Horta •

Vulci
(Ponte della Badia) •

Castel d'Asso •

Norchia •

Lake
Vico

Falerii •

Graviscae
(Lido di
Tarquinia) •

Blera •

Nepeta •

Tarquinii
(Tarquinia)

Sutrium •

Lake
Bracciano

River Tiber

Caere (Cerveteri) •

Pyrgi •

Veii (Vejo) •

Alsium
(Palo) •

Rome •

MEDITERRANEAN

LATIUM

RIVER PO

Bologna •

ADRIATIC SEA

R. ARNO

CORSICA

R. TIBER

LATIUM

SARDINIA

Herculaneum •

Pompeii •

Etruria

SICILY

113

villages between the River Po to the north, the Tiber to the south, the Apennines to the east, and the sea to the west. This whole area was densely populated, as we know from the vestiges of walls, roads, drainage tunnels, and tombs; and, indeed, from the remains of cities like Fidenae, Sutrium, Falerii, Nepete, Horta, Blera, Norchia, and others that were not included on the list of the Twelve. Yet all of these places, judging by the remains, were extensive and populous urban centres. Still other communities, either mentioned by classical writers or evidenced by their monuments, have never been identified or systematically excavated, though the extent of the cemeteries that surround them indicate that they were places of importance. Yet again, there are Etruscan towns which some scholars maintain are purely mythical, and others claim to have actually discovered. Such is Corythus, said to have been named after a legendary hero, Corythus, son of Paris. George Dennis was sure that he had found Corythus at Cortona. 'Yon solemn city,' he writes, 'was once the proudest and mightiest in the land, the metropolis of Etruria, and now – but enter its gates and look around.' He entered himself, but hurriedly retired on account of his experience at the inn, Il Dragone, 'a wretched osteria, full of uncleanliness'. However, he found clean lodgings down the steep hill from Cortona, and set to work in his usual thorough manner to explore the town, its outlying tombs, and the treasures acquired by the local treasure hunters, certain that he had found the lost Etruscan Corythus. But Etruscologists today cannot agree with him. They say that if the place existed at all, it was more likely somewhere in the neighbourhood of Tarquinia, some sixty miles to the south of Cortona. Similar disagreement is voiced as to the location of cities like Caletra (Pitigliano? Marsigliana d'Albegna?), Malpum, famed for its wealth, and many others whose names are completely unknown. Yet the importance of some of them, if only to their own citizens, is indicated by the fact that they often minted their own coins which have come down to us bearing names like Peithesa and Echelia, otherwise unidentifiable. Such is the extent of our ignorance of the number, importance, and location of the Etruscan places.

ABOVE Many Etruscan cities minted their own coins, including Populonia (top) and Volterra (middle and bottom).

Such, too, is our reason for assuming that there never was a nation called Etruria, with a central government and twelve distinct regional capitals. Rather, there were evidently fifty or more large and wealthy cities whose only real interests in common were their religious, cultural, and linguistic ties. Of these three bonds, the first welded the people together more than any political or commercial alliance, as is shown by the annual festival held at the national shrine of the god Voltumna and attended by the heads of state. The location of this shrine, the *fanum Voltumnae*, is still unknown – another indication of our ignorance of things Etruscan, and also a clue that the sanctuary was not the site of a magnificent temple like the Greek ones at Paestum, but a 'sacred grove', the kind of Arcadian retreat so beloved of those pagans who worshipped God in his natural rather than his anthropomorphic manifestations. Concerning the god Voltumna we know little. He was perhaps one of those ancient father figures like Zeus, who was more of a national symbol than a living force, and his festival no doubt originated as a thanksgiving service which the Etruscan emigrants may have held after they landed safely on the west coast of Italy. In the early days of the Confederation, the leaders of the various clans took the opportunity of the Voltumnan gathering to discuss their problems and to settle differences with one another. Evidently, too, in times of emergency the clan chieftains elected one of their members as their commander-in-chief or president, no doubt choosing a man of advanced age and one renowned for his wisdom and virtue.

This arrangement worked well enough as long as the Etruscan city-states had no national enemies, but it appears to have been wholly inadequate in times of crisis. For already by the fifth century B.C. the Gaulish barbarians were envious of their civilized neighbours in northern Italy and in the immemorial manner of barbarians, attacked and destroyed what they envied. The Confederation of the Twelve does not appear to have worked out any policy for national defence in this time of extreme danger, nor do the cities seem to have united in organized resistance to the invaders. And soon after, a new and even more dangerous enemy than the Gauls threatened the security of the Etruscans, namely the Romans who had also observed the prosperity of their rivals and particularly

BELOW A typical cinerary urn from Volterra. The frieze depicts a battle between the Etruscans and barbarians.

LEFT Bronze figurine of an Etruscan warrior of the mid-5th century B.C. These little figurines were made in large numbers as votive offerings. MIDDLE Bronze statuette of a flautist playing the double pipes. RIGHT Bronze figurine of a dancer supporting a candelabrum on her head. 5th century B.C.

116

that of the near-by city of Veii. Thus there arose two basic causes of war – the first being the age-old envy of the underdeveloped countries for civilized states; the second, the problems caused by over-population. Rome, then, by the end of the fifth century B.C. had grown to the extent that its population could not be adequately housed and fed, whence the only solution was the acquisition of somebody else's territory. The nearest such land to Rome was held by the Etruscans of Veii, and to the Romans the conquest of this territory soon became a matter of life or death. Livy records fourteen separate wars; the last was a ten-year siege of the city of Veii, which was finally captured by means of the famous *cuniculus*, or Mine of Camillus. This mine was actually a tunnel dug through the rock on which stood the citadel of Veii. The legend has it that the Roman sappers tunnelling night and day finally brought their shaft to a point below the floor of the Temple of Juno where the High Priest was making a sacrifice and the augur was examining the entrails of the sacrificed animal. Confident under the circumstances (that is, taking a reasonable gamble in view of the lack of success of the enemy over such a long period), the Etruscan sooth-sayer prophesied that whoever laid the entrails of the sacrifice on the altar would be victorious. Hearing this, the Roman commandos, who were awaiting orders to break out, burst from under the pavement of the temple, seized the entrails, and rushed back to their commander, Marcus Furius Camillus, who completed the sacrificial rite himself while his troops poured into the city and subjected it to the inevitable fate of classical sieges. So fell Veii after three hundred years of resisting Roman aggression.

There is no need to disbelieve this story in its entirety. Historians have learned that nearly all legends contain a kernel of truth, and the truth here seems to be that Veii was finally lost from within, whether because of the Roman siege tunnel (which has never been found) or because of treachery. For some sort of collusion must be the explanation of the surrender of so many high-walled and seemingly impregnable Etruscan cities, falling to the Romans one by one, often without even a token resistance, as in the case of Sutrium, until by the end of the first century B.C. the whole of Etruria was in Roman hands and the Etruscans no longer existed as a separate and independent people. Indeed, the Emperor Claudius was writing about them in A.D. 30 as though they already belonged to history despite the fact that pockets of true Etruscans, still speaking their native language, survived in remote country places. The Etruscan Discipline, too, became an integral part of Roman theology, though it is doubtful whether any educated Romans took haruspicy, the Etruscan speciality, very seriously. In fact, by Claudius's time almost everything essentially Etruscan had been destroyed, forgotten, or entombed in the earth.

It is no wonder, therefore, that the professional Etruscologists, like the Roman historians, cannot agree even as to which of the principal Etruscan cities actually formed the Etruscan league. All agree that there were twelve such cities, but

LEFT Breastplate of an Etruscan heavy-armed warrior. MIDDLE Villanovan bronze helmet. The Villanovans were the Iron Age people who occupied the area of central Italy settled by the Etruscans. RIGHT A victor's helmet of the 7th century B.C. decorated with ivy leaves and berries.

neither they nor the modern writers concur as to their names. It has to be assumed, therefore, that each city was an independent community ruled over by a chief magistrate called a *lucumo*, which Latin writers translate as *princeps* and which we, in turn would translate as 'head of state'. The state itself was a theocracy: its laws, national policies, and rituals were all determined by the celebrated Etruscan Discipline. The essence of this code was that the destiny of men as of nations was predetermined by the will of the gods whose decisions were constantly being sought out and, where possible, anticipated. It follows that such a society could not conceive of democracy in its modern sense. Indeed, the Etruscans would have been appalled by our political practices, in which men jostle for authority and power without reference to the will of the gods. They accepted as irrevocable the divine plan by which every man's life was pre-destined. Such submission to the gods meant acceptance of authority on earth, since the priest-kings of the theocracies were the representatives of those gods, interpreting the divine will and presenting it to the populace in the form of decrees from heaven. Sometimes those decrees came down from above inscribed on tablets of stone or bronze, as the legal code of the Babylonian Hammurabi and the Commandments of the Israelite Moses were deposited on mountain-tops. And sometimes they were read in portents divined from natural phenomena – the clap of thunder, the flash of lightning, the flight of birds, or the state of the liver of a newly sacrificed sheep.

Yet however god-conscious the Etruscans were, they were at the same time a very worldly race. Nor was there necessarily anything contradictory in their attitudes, since they argued that if their whole life with its hopes and fears, its chances of happiness and its certainty of suffering, were beyond their control, they had the right to enjoy every moment of time that they could, even though fate was watching and waiting, ready to destroy them if they were too happy. And so we should perhaps think of the ordinary Etruscan as an outwardly pious man who never questioned either the existence or the omnipotence of the gods yet, by virtue of his resultant intellectual diffidence, was the opposite of the Christian mystic with his creed of self-denial. Manifestly, the Etruscans surrounded themselves with all the good things of life they could acquire.

Indeed, it was their insatiable demand for luxuries that stimulated a brisk international trade all over the Mediterranean, a commerce dealing principally in non-utilitarian goods: bronzes, statues, painted vases, jewellery, and ornaments made in the ateliers of Greek craftsmen and exported by the ship-load to Etruria. And even after they had partially lost control of the central Mediterranean waters to the Greek and Carthaginian navies, they continued a brisk export-import business which made them the richest nation of the Italian peninsula and, indeed, one of the richest nations of the entire world in the eighth century B.C. There can be no other explanation for the enormous quantities of treasure unearthed wherever the Etruscans had cities, large or small. Tens of thousands of vases imported from Greece and vases made in local potteries; every sort of jewellery from gold safety pins to exquisitely engraved necklaces; all the utensils needed for a luxurious house – cauldrons, wine bowls, jugs, basins, pails, plates, cups, vessels of every shape and size, not to mention furniture, weapons, and armour, have been found. One is reminded of the quantities of Victorian articles and *objets d'art* which are today finding their way into the antique market; the supply seems inexhaustible as the supply of Etruscan artefacts must have seemed unlimited in the nineteenth century. Such wealth could only have been created by tremendous industry at home and a well-organized trade abroad, which encouraged the free flow of goods all over the civilized world, the finest Greek vases, for instance, being sent to Etruria and Etruscan bronzes being exported to Greece. Certainly no nation of the ancient world – or, for that matter, of the modern world – surpassed the Etruscans in bronze work. Nearly all the articles they manufactured in this metal are pure works of art, whether they are simple household utensils like cauldrons, colanders, cups, pails, fire rakes, or ornaments like the exquisite chaplets of laurel and ivy leaves worn, as we see from the tomb paintings, at banquets: all are examples of a culture conditioned by a love and respect for beauty. One wonders why these designs are not copied by modern manufacturers of household articles.

Such a thriving commerce between nations implies the existence of a specific merchant class with its traders, shippers, brokers, and middlemen. The same mercantile community must have flourished in old Babylon and in the capitals of all the Near and Middle Eastern empires, though unfortunately we hear little about these businessmen and their activities. Yet it was the Arab traders who first made contact with the civilizations of the Far East from which they must have brought back many ideas and skills which influenced western civilization. So too, though much later in time, it was the Jewish commercial travellers who carried the story and gospel of the New Messiah to the cities all round the Mediterranean shores. But businessmen were not part of the official establishment in either Babylon or Etruria, and since they never formed a class, like the priests at one extreme and the slaves at the other, we must assume that they were neutral men, very much behind the scenes, concerned primarily with

TOP Terracotta frieze from an Etruscan temple of the 5th century B.C., depicting a scene from Greek mythology. No Etruscan temples have survived, since they were built of unbaked brick, wood, and other perishable materials.

BOTTOM Alabaster urn from the necropolis of Cortona. Local Etruscan artists often depicted on the sides of burial urns scenes from the life of the deceased or his family's grief at his departure.

OVERLEAF Golden goblet from the Barberini tomb at Palestrina (Praeneste), depicting date palms and people working in the fields. The strong Egyptian influence and motifs of the gold, silver, and bronze treasures taken from the Palestrina tombs date these finds to the 7th century B.C.

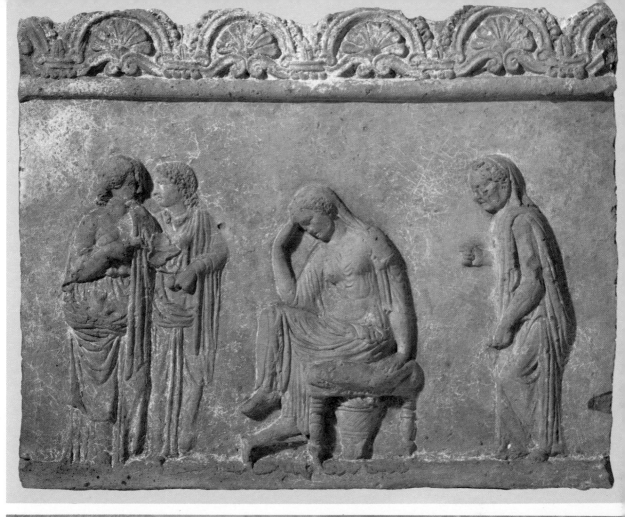

Two warriors carrying a dead comrade. The group forms the handle of the lid of a bronze cista and typifies a frequently used feature of Etruscan containers.

making money. And since there was no such thing as political parties, they had no voice in the government of the country and probably wanted none.

The same was true of the military, though in any case the Etruscans appear not to have had a standing army, so we cannot really speak of a soldier class. We have to remember that warfare in the Mediterranean world of the eighth century B.C. was as much a private as a national enterprise and that armies were as often as not in the service of local barons rather than of kings. The earliest Etruscans whose names we know, from the records or legends – Porsena, the Tarquins, the Vibenna brothers, Mastarna, and a few others – were probably independent guerrilla leaders who lived by plunder and looting. As long as these freebooters did not interfere with the prosperity of their native cities, but, on the contrary, added to it by gifts and thanksgiving offerings, they were regarded as great heroes and patriots, rather like Sir Francis Drake and other pirates of the Elizabethan period were regarded by the common people of England. Moreover, it was probably the private armies of these chieftains which accounted for the actual territorial conquests of the early Etruscans. Well-armed mercenaries under the leadership of some experienced general would have no difficulty in subduing the barbarians they encountered on their excursions in search of plunder (cattle, women, and grain); and if the country thus subdued was rich in natural resources, the developers, the merchants, and farmers with their slaves would quickly move in and so establish another centre of civilization in barbarian territory. In this manner the Etruscan dominion eventually spread as far north as the Po Valley and as far south as Naples.

Yet despite the extent of their empire, the Etruscan city-states were obliged to fall back in times of emergency on an archaic convention whereby every man who was called to the colours was required to name another recruit. This was no doubt an expedient way in which to muster practically the entire population of the country, but it is certain that men conscripted in this fashion were neither willing volunteers nor experienced professionals. No wonder that the Etruscan armies were doomed to be defeated and practically annihilated on the field of battle, sixty thousand of them falling to the Romans at the Battle of the Ciminian Forest in 310 B.C., a further massacre befalling them at the Battle of Lake Vadimon two years later, still another at Rusellae (Roselle, near Grosseto) in 303 B.C., and so on until in 280 B.C. the last stronghold of the Etruscans – the city of the central Etruscan shrine, Volsinii – fell to the Roman Consul, Tiberius Coruncanius. And with Volsinii fell the entire Etruscan system, the theocratic and patrician hierarchy based on the Etruscan Discipline, or sacred law.[1] The system collapsed after one of those rare occasions in which the slaves somehow managed to organize a nation-wide revolt. Any such rebellion was doomed to failure, as Spartacus and his fellow gladiators were to discover in 71 B.C., but the Etruscan serfs of Volsinii came nearer to success than the Roman slaves and seemed for a time to have succeeded after they had seized

[1] See Chapter Eight for a detailed discussion.

control of the city, murdered the most hated of their masters, abused the wives and daughters of slave owners, and plundered the houses of the rich. Their reign of terror was short, however, for the patricians who had managed to escape from the city called upon the Roman army to save them, and this was, of course, done with great expedition. The rebellious slaves were liquidated, the surviving nobles transferred to Rome with what wealth they had managed to conceal, and the last of the Etruscan cities was razed to the ground.

Aerial view of the Etruscan port of Spina on the Adriatic. The photograph shows that the city was built in a chessboard pattern.

What the course of history would have been if the Etruscans had had the political acumen to unite as a nation instead of relying on a loose confederation of their richer cities is, of course, mere speculation. But one could imagine that with a properly trained and disciplined *national* army commensurate with their wealth, they might have emerged victorious in the long struggle with Rome and so have become the masters of the whole of Italy. But the evidence suggests that they were not a warrior people like the restless Gauls to the north and the ambitious Romans to the south. Alternatively, it is arguable that their rigid system, so intrinsically hostile to political or social change, led to their inevitably being overtaken by their more dynamic neighbours. History appears to offer comparable cases of monolithic states distinguished for their intellectual obscurantism being swept away by peoples uninhibited by inflexible religious and political creeds. One recalls the civilizations of Mesopotamia which used their science not in the cause of human advancement but in the service of divine anthropomorphs, as the Babylonians used their immense knowledge of astronomy. It is, therefore, possible that the Etruscans – with their obsession with fate, their reliance on omens, and the resultant charlatanism of their religion –

were always at a disadvantage in confronting a practical enemy like the Romans. And, though it is true that the latter people eventually adopted the famous Etruscan Discipline with its secrets of divination, one doubts whether a Roman as ruthless as Camillus, conqueror of Veii, actually believed in all the mumbo-jumbo that this system involved. Is it credible, for instance, that a Roman commander, having worked out his strategy and tactics for a critical campaign, would be dissuaded from putting his plan into action on account of some priest drawing his attention to the defects in the flukes of a sheep's liver? No, the Romans, like the Greeks, accepted the fact of godhead and regarded its recognition as a civic responsibility; but neither people ever bowed down in abject fear to their gods, or believed that their struggle against hostile forces was utterly hopeless, or relied for salvation, national or private, on the incantations of priests.

But if a submissive attitude in religion was characteristic of the nations of the Near and Middle East, so, too, was the love of pleasure and luxury, which was one of the reasons the stern Roman moralists of the Republic seized upon to denounce a people they intended to attack and, if possible, destroy. Their disdain is implicit in their jibes about 'fat Etruscans'; and judging from the portly gentlemen reclining on the lids of sarcophagi, the wealthy and well fed Etruscan nobles tended in middle age to a Near Eastern corpulence. But in view of the gloom and terrors of their religious creed with its hideous monsters like the monkey-faced and flaming-eyed Charun, who is armed with a mallet to crush

OVERLEAF A funerary chest with banqueting scenes, typical of those found in many Etruscan tombs. About 470 B.C.

ABOVE Scarab of carnelian with a miniature of the Trojan Horse.

RIGHT War elephant followed by a calf. Decoration on an Etruscan plate dated to the mid-3rd century B.C. It is the only representation of an elephant ever found in Etruria.

127

the skull of the newly deceased, it is no wonder that the Etruscans opted for a good life here on earth.

They obtained such a life by organizing their creature comforts along sound engineering and technological lines. No great builders in stone except for defence purposes, they created comfortable houses of sun-dried brick and timber, emphasizing function rather than aesthetics. Heating, hydraulics, and drainage were given careful attention; and it is evident from what remains of of their cities (as distinct from their cemeteries) that the Etruscans were the most advanced sanitary and civil engineers in the ancient world. The quality of life in their dominions is, in any case, attested to by the fact that all of Etruria was densely populated – abounding in major cities, market towns, villages, farms, and rich agricultural estates. The same countryside two thousand five hundred years later was almost completely deserted, ravaged by malaria, and abandoned to those animals that know how to survive in marshy fenland. George Dennis saw this landscape during his mid-nineteenth-century travels and called it a 'wilderness from which man hurries away as from a plague-stricken land'. Yet so fertile was this region that the Romans used to receive consignments of corn from the Etruscans in times of famine throughout Latium.

Prosperous and comfortable in their homes, the well-born Etruscans could enjoy the fruits of their technical achievements and the labour of their underlings. Their chief pleasures revolved round various festive occasions, notably the celebrated open-air banquets which were such a feature of all social life throughout the pre-Christian Mediterranean world. Perhaps the best wall paintings in the tombs are those depicting these banquets, for the artists have captured that spirit of gaiety which so shocked the Greeks and later, though for different reasons, the Romans. The former people disapproved not because of the abundance of food and drink that were obviously consumed, nor because of the presence of dancing girls and musicians, for they enjoyed all these accompaniments of a banquet themselves. We meet Socrates at one such evening party at the house of the Syracusan Callias where he was delighted with a dancing girl's acrobatic performance. No, the Greeks were shocked by the presence of the host's wife and his guests' wives at the Etruscan feasts, for this offended their peculiar moral code, by which respectable women (wives and daughters) lived out their lives behind the scenes, almost precisely as in strict Muslim communities. The only women who appeared in public were courtesans, and therefore when the Greek observers of Etruscan customs noted that an Etruscan man and woman attending a banquet were at table under the same covering, they automatically assumed that this pair were making love in public. Again, while the Greeks saw no sin in the naked body, either of men or women, they had set rules about where one exposed oneself – in the gymnasium or in the boxing ring, for instance, and among one's fellow athletes, but not at a dinner party. But the Etruscans, according to the fourth-century B.C. historian, Theopompus

130

A plaque showing the deceased riding through the Underworld in a chariot. The scene below represents him as a cavalryman fighting a Gaul on foot. The Gauls were sometimes enemies and sometimes friends of the Etruscans.

of Chios, were a scandalously immoral people, since men and women exercised naked in the gymnasium together, dined together, and – worst of all – drank together. In fact, the women drank more than the men, so that it was scarcely surprising after eating, drinking, and sitting on a man's lap at table that the diners coupled openly after the banquet. So, at any rate, says Theopompus, though we note that this observer, according to some of his contemporaries, was the sort of ill-tempered old man who took more pleasure in reviling than in praising his fellow men.

The tomb paintings seem partially to confirm the account given by Theo-pompus, for women are indeed seen lying beside their male companions, exchanging tasty morsels of food as a sign of affection and, in some cases, leaning languorously on a husband's or lover's breast. The women, however, are usually elegantly dressed, as beautiful clothes and jewellery were an important attribute of pleasure to the Etruscans, just as they were symptomatic of decadence to the Roman moralists. The men, on the other hand, were bare to the waist, a naked torso evidently being *de rigueur* for banquets. Indeed, the men wore as little as they needed in order to keep warm, for we see the male servants scuttling back and forth with pitchers of wine always naked; and even horsemen wear nothing but a short cloak. Both sexes adorned themselves with laurel wreaths and necklaces of flowers. Ballerinas wore diaphanous dresses, knowing instinctively that they were much more sexually exciting when semi-concealed in this manner than if they had been completely naked, as Greek girl dancers frequently were. There is no doubt, then, that an Etruscan banquet was a very lively and gay affair; and judging from the fact that it was painted in the tombs, it must have represented one aspect of paradise to these hedonists of central Italy; that is, an eternity of eating, drinking, dancing, and loving to the music of the pipe and harp.

Theopompus the Greek was, of course, really condemning the Etruscans for being different from the Greeks – especially in their regard for and treatment of women. For whereas the Greeks, despite all their science, philosophy, and art, had degraded women to a level not much higher than that of bond slaves, the Etruscans had raised women to a position of dignity complementary to that of their menfolk. Hence the presence of wives and lovers at the banquet, the simulacrum of the wife on the funeral monument, she side by side and some-times hand in hand with her spouse, not reduced in size, as on the Crusaders' tombs, but his equal and his companion in public as in private. Hence, too, the portraits of women holding writing tablets, proof that girls went to school the same as the boys and had the same advantage in later life of being able to read and write. All this was in contrast to the enslavement of women in Greece during the fourth century B.C. when Theopompus was accusing the Etruscans of immorality, intemperance, and a too permissive society.

A Gorgon's head from a water pot found in a tomb at Tarquinia. The monster-gargoyles on medieval cathedrals are the direct descendants of these Etruscan fetishes.

The Romans adopted this Greek attitude of righteous indignation in their

TOP Cortona today – the ruins of the 5th-century B.C. Etruscan walls, rebuilt in Roman times. Cortona, which claims to be the oldest city in Italy, is the headquarters of the Accademia Etrusca, founded in the mid-18th century.

BOTTOM View of Lake Trasimene, scene of the defeat of the Roman army by Hannibal in 217 B.C.

turn, although their hostility towards their rivals for the mastery of Italy was more immediate and personal. Etruscan decadence, they said, was due to luxurious living and the constant pursuit of pleasure instead of plain living. This charge is made quite clear in a long detailed description of Etruscan manners by the Sicilian historian Diodorus, who was a Roman in outlook even though a Greek by birth and education.[1] Diodorus, then, maintains that prosperity brought the Etruscans to their decline – a very facile and, for all we know, valid explanation of the fall of empires and kingdoms throughout history. The Etruscan fields, says the historian, were altogether too fertile, their farming too efficient, their harvests too abundant. This superabundance of the good things of life naturally led to intemperance, typified by the two sumptuous meals a day served on beautifully appointed tables alongside which men and women reclined at their ease, garlanded with laurel leaves and fresh flowers, to be served on silver plates and from silver goblets and entertained by musicians and dancers. And even worse, continues Diodorus, the slaves who waited at table were richly attired despite their condition of servitude; and he concluded that all this luxury and abundance of the good things of life led to the loss of the ancient martial spirit which had once made Etruria feared by the whole world.

A decidedly less sensational explanation of the decline and fall of the Etruscan *imperium* is found in the hints scattered here and there in the Roman histories of the manner in which the principal cities were conquered one by one and the price they paid for defeat. Veii, after decades of guerrilla warfare as the city on the very frontiers of Rome, was the first to fall. The final campaign, as we have seen, lasted ten years, though it is obvious that the siege of Veii by the Roman army actually consisted of a series of border clashes which made very little difference to life in either city. In other words, the war was not between the ordinary citizens but between landowners and their private armies. The Roman citizens encouraged these endless attacks on the Veiian territories since their own lands had become infertile and incapable of supporting the expanding population.

But even when Veii was being really hard pressed by the Roman battalions, the other cities of the Confederation did little to help their ally. Why?

The fact that we cannot answer this important question positively is another indication of our ignorance of the Etruscan political system. Why, for instance, did the cities of Central Etruria allow their compatriots in the north to be overrun by the Gauls and those to the south by the Romans? Their indifference could not have been due to a failure of communications, since the beleaguered cities appealed to the Confederation for help but received none.

We can only assume that, apart from a common language and a common cultural heritage, the citizens of the various Etruscan communities had no concept of nationhood. Their nation was their city; its surrounding farmlands their country. As long as these were not threatened, they were not concerned with the fate of towns and regions which lay beyond their horizon. Consequently, the

[1] Diodorus Siculus, *Bibliotheca Historica*, V, 40.

135

Etruscans were not conquered as a nation at all; they were dismembered, as it were, town by town, by sporadic incursions into their territory. The Gauls, for their part, invaded in the hope of loot. They knew from whence came the good things of life which, as barbarians, they were unable to produce themselves – the gold ornaments, splendid weapons, elegant furniture and furnishings, cultivated fruits, and delicious wines of the Italian plains. The portly Etruscan burghers with their militia of serfs were no match for the hordes of Celts who poured out of the north and passed across the country like clouds of locusts, only stopping, or being stopped, when they came up against high walls and rock-girt citadels. The Etruscan policy was to withdraw behind the walls of their cities and if the barbarians dislocated their agriculture and commerce too seriously, to attempt to buy them off. In addition, they entered into alliances wherever they could, irrespective of the credentials of their new ally. Some Etruscan cities, for instance, made military pacts with Rome against the Gauls, even though the Romans were systematically destroying or annexing their sister communities. Others made alliances with the Gauls against the Romans. It was, of course, the politics of opportunism whereby the hated enemies of yesterday became the allies of tomorrow. There is, however, nothing unusual in the diplomatic manoeuvrings by which the Etruscans attempted to ensure their survival.

Unfortunately for them their tactics did not succeed, since no matter what alien ally they chose, there was no loyalty and no trust among their own compatriots. In the end, when it was already too late to unite against the Romans for one last stand, the Etruscan leaders of a number of cities made secret agreements with the Roman commanders, allowing them to take possession of cities which were regarded as expendable. So fell Sutrium, Fidenae, and finally Volsinii, the religious centre and heart of Etruria.

Do the facts that we have – all of them derived from the Roman commentators – adequately explain the collapse of such a rich and powerful people as the Etruscans? Were they so unwarlike and, indeed, supine that they surrendered their cities without any sort of resistance? It is possible, for several reasons, to reject this hypothesis. Even the Romans admitted that the Etruscans fought bravely and even fanatically in the last great battle at the Vadimon Lake. But it is possible that they fought without hope, as they seem to have done in the last days of Veii when the omens went against them. The end in their view had already been written, and even though they tried by peering into the entrails of sacrificial animals to learn what it was, they seem to have been convinced that they could do nothing to change it. In the last analysis, their view of life seemed to derive from a philosophy of despair, epitomized by their religion and its emphasis on the implacable decrees of fate.

CHAPTER EIGHT

Religion

I T IS DIFFICULT for us today to understand the role of religion in Etruscan life since the relationship of God to man and the part the divine plays in mundane affairs are no longer of paramount importance to the majority of men and women in the western world. Political, economic, and even social decisions are made without any consultation with a god, even if an official deity is overtly addressed on important public occasions and his approval is requested for what is going to be done in any case, whether that be the prosecution of a war or the erection of a building. It could indeed be argued that nothing distinguishes the ancient and medieval worlds from the modern one more than this attitude towards godhead, for while societies from the Sumerians to the European kingdoms of the fourteenth century could not have functioned without an integration of church and state, modern western societies function on exactly the opposite principle. The more advanced we become, the less we depend on divine intervention.

One reason for dispensing with a god appears to be that, since our calculations are based on fixed laws of mechanics, our expectations of happiness, not to mention survival, no longer depend on our success in placating an unseen power. With the aid of science, the agnostic will undertake to explain why a good person, or an innocent child, or an expectant mother is struck down by a stray bullet while the evil or old or useless are spared: it has all to do with the laws of physics. The Etruscans, however, could accept no such interpretation. For them the inequalities and injustices of existence were only explicable as originating from the intervention of celestial beings who governed the cosmos by laws which were not fully understood and which it was therefore futile to dispute.

The resultant fatalism which is so characteristic of all early religions had been long manifested in the various cults of pre-Etruscan peoples, and one has only to open the Bible at the book of Job to glimpse the extent of this total submission to the will of the god. On the other hand, with non-Semitic races, to which the Etruscans may have belonged, there were at least some prospects of respite, if not of any great hope, in the pagan view of life. There was not simply one god, stern and relentless, who demanded preposterous sacrifices, as Abraham imagined Jahweh demanded of him. There were many gods, scores of them, together with their consorts, paramours, sons and daughters, and a variety of demi-gods like the nymphs and dryads who dwelt in trees, fountains, and waterfalls. In fact, there were so many of them that a great deal of their time was spent in harassing each other instead of their subjects on earth below. Even so, they were constantly involved in every human activity, always present, either on earth, or in their celestial habitations from which they could observe the goings-on of the earth below. The sceptical Greeks made a fairy tale world out of this complex theogony, and certainly some of the most charming poetry, both Greek and Latin, resulted from the contemplation of this idyllic country beyond mortal frontiers. Conversely, serious-minded Greeks, like the writers of tragedy, questioned the justice of the gods and the desirability of man's bondage to them. But the divine essence and the close interrelationship between gods and men were always acknowledged even by the greatest of the philosophers, by none more so than Socrates, the man accused of atheism.

The Etruscans in their relationship with the divine seem to have had neither the fantasy nor the philosophy of the Greeks, nor, for that matter, the practicality of the Romans. Their gods were, of course, anthropomorphs, for they could hardly be anything else if one was genuinely to believe in them, since once the theologian begins to argue whether god is a force or a spirit of some sort or the other, deity ceases to exist except as a philosophical or ethical abstraction, of no interest to a worshipper who needs some tangible proof of, as well as contact with, his celestial lord. The Etruscan gods, then, were either anthropomorphs or quasi-mythical monsters in common with all the other gods of the ancient world; and they were a numerous as well as a curious collection. It is inevitable that we do not altogether understand who they were, where they came from, and what they did. Some of them appear to be of Hellenic origin, or at least to have Greek names: Hercle for Herakles (Hercules), Aplu for Apollo, Aritimi for Artemis. But this does not prove at all that the Etruscans borrowed these gods from the Greek pantheon, for in the first place, gods are not borrowed from rival religions: they are imposed by edict, as the Christian God was imposed on the pagan Romans by the Edict of Milan; or they are introduced by immigrants or outsiders, or cliques of one sort or another. In the second place, gods like Hercules, Apollo, and Artemis were far older than Hellenic civilization and belonged to a period so far back in history that we only have glimpses of it in the prehistoric art of southern Europe and Africa.

Of these man-gods worshipped by the ancients, Hercules is the most interesting since he symbolizes the most deep-seated of religious feelings: namely, the longing for a human champion who will challenge the celestial despots on behalf of weak and helpless mortals. For it is axiomatic that in the end most gods are tyrants, because there is no other explanation of the gratuitous misery and suffering they inflict upon even the most blameless of mortals, so many of whom (like new-born babes) are utterly innocent of wrongdoing and therefore not deserving

Silver mask engraved with stylized figures of birds and cabalistic signs. It was found covering the face of a corpse in an Etruscan tomb.

of punishment in the form of sickness, pain, or death. Hercules, then, appears as man's champion in one form or another in all early religions, even as far back as the Sumerians, by whom he was called Gilgamesh. From the Sumerians the *mythus* of a folk hero spread throughout the Middle and the Near East, and from there to the entire Mediterranean world, because here was one man-god with whom ordinary mortals could identify, whereas the thunder gods like Zeus in his various manifestations and the destroyers like Apollo in his were completely alien and unsympathetic, even though they all had to be placated and paid tribute to exactly like the mortal tyrant kings who resembled them. But Hercules, whom we know best in his Hellenic form, championed the oppressed and timorous by his famous labours, freeing men from the threat of wild beasts – lions, sea monsters, and the like – and from various human monsters like Diomedes, the Thracian King who fed his horses on human flesh. And in a more mystical sense he laboured to conquer the terrors of death itself, by descending into Hell and surviving the journey. His heroic life, in brief, gave men some hope and some identification with at least one of the gods, and this undoubtedly accounts for the universality of Hercules-worship. The Etruscans worshipped him too, and could well have brought him with them from Lydia, where the great hero spent some time at the court of the Lydian Queen, Omphale. The

LEFT Lycian tomb probably built for a Persian or Lycian prince about 375 B.C. Lycia, the neighbouring state to Lydia, was the original home of Apollo, adopted as Aplu by the Etruscans.

RIGHT A rhyton, or drinking cup, the original form of which was an animal's horn. Here the potter has perhaps deliberately caricatured the death demon, Charun.

story typifies the Lydian mentality: Hercules was tamed by this regal woman and, to please her, wore her clothes while she strutted around in his. We see in this legend – as in the Etruscan myth of Juno giving suck to Hercules, who is portrayed in the Volterra mirror as a bearded man leaning nonchalantly on the arm of the goddess's chair while he takes her nipple in his mouth – the oriental approval of that femininity which softened the harshness of a world dominated by tyrannical gods and men.

Aplu, too, was probably originally a folk hero like Hercules, who sided with mortals in their eternal struggle against the hostile forces of the cosmos. Aplu, or Apollo as the Greeks knew him, is Lycian in provenance, and as Lycia was the neighbouring state to Lydia, the gods and goddesses, their cults and rituals, were more or less interchangeable. Like Hercules, Aplu rid mankind of various monsters and tyrants and was loved for this reason. The Etruscans regarded him as a paragon of male beauty, softened by that same humanity they found in Hercules at the court of Queen Omphale; and they have left us a representation of their god which enables us to understand their thoughts and feelings. The statue of Apollo which was found in the ruins of Veii is the portrait of a sensual, mysteriously smiling young aristocrat who is the diametric opposite of the great bearded statues of the senior gods.

The other Etruscan gods could be called the standardized deities of the early Mediterranean world, and we know little about them or about their worship. They appear to have been anthropomorphs from as far back as Sumerian times

Wall painting from the Tomb of Orcus, Tarquinia. Hades (the Etruscan Aita), enthroned with Persephone (Phersipnai), is addressing the triple-headed god Geryon (Cerun).

and to have survived as relics of a succession of theocentric societies, passed along from Sumer to Babylon to Assyria, and so to all parts of the oriental world. Most of these gods and their offspring were given a place in the established church, which conducted its business like any secular department of government, with its ministries, civil servants, and administrative offices. It is likely that the average Etruscan felt little personal involvement with many of these deities except in so far as he was conditioned to accept their will as the inscrutable decree of fate. And to this extent agnosticism, like atheism, was unthinkable. But the gods were omnipotent, omniscient, and omnipresent. They planned every moment of a man's life, from the cradle to the grave: hence it was useless to struggle against one's destiny or to complain about one's misfortunes. All the individual could do was to hope for some amelioration of his lot if he found, as it were, the right combination to put him in touch with one or the other of the gods. From earliest times the priests had a monopoly in this skill, which they took good care to shroud in ever denser veils of mystery. Indeed, it is possible that the Etruscan priests, like certain modern specialists, did not themselves understand the intricacies of their science, for there appears to be considerable confusion in the

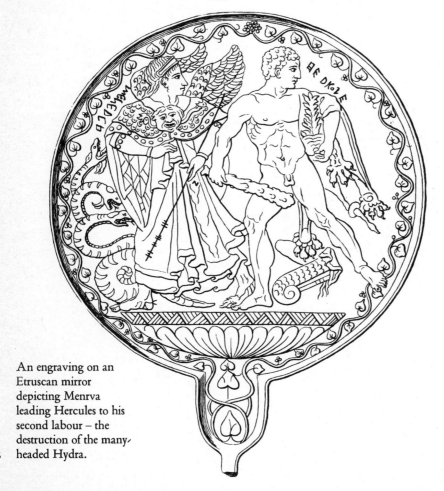

An engraving on an Etruscan mirror depicting Menrva leading Hercules to his second labour – the destruction of the many-headed Hydra.

names and functions of the diverse gods, some of whom, like the shrouded gods (*Dii involuti*), could not be identified at all; others like the twelve great gods, six of each sex, could not be named; and still others, the nine thunderbolt-hurling gods, for instance, becoming mixed up as to the time and place at which they let loose their celestial artillery.

From this it can be seen that a highly specialized priesthood was required in precisely the same manner and for the same reasons that the modern secular state requires a specialized civil service. The priests, then, formed the nucleus of the government, for they were the holy men who had received the sacred testament at the founding of the nation and who had transmitted the text of divine doctrine to their descendants. This doctrine was, in fact, the political as well as the spiritual constitution of Etruria – the famous *Disciplina Etrusca* which distinguished the Confederation from all other contemporary states and gave the Etruscans the reputation of being the most pious people of their time.

We may refer to the *Disciplina* as a bible or sacred testament in that it was said to be divinely inspired and therefore the ultimate authority on earth. Where did this Etruscan bible come from? Unlike those testaments which were brought

A prototype of the love goddess, variously called Aphrodite, Astarte, and Venus; the Etruscans named her Turan.

Etruscan mirror engraved with the figures of (left to right) Aplu (spelled Apulu), Tinia, and Cadmus.

143

down from heaven and delivered to a national leader (the Code to Hammurabi; the Commandments to Moses; the Golden Tablets to Joseph Smith), the Etruscan legend has a chthonian origin. The sacred laws were given to Tarchon, the leader of the Etruscans, not by a celestial messenger who floated down from heaven, but by a hobgoblin called Tages, a little old dwarf who crawled out of the ground and dictated twelve books of religious law. Why the Etruscan myth-makers should have chosen this misshapen mannikin as the author of their rule of life is puzzling, unless it was the result of their obsession with the underworld. Tages, then, even though he had been turned up, like a worm, by the plough, was the patron divinity of all Etruria, since it was he who gave the nation a doctrine which regulated every aspect of public life and, even more than that, a tradition which bound all the Etruscan cities together in bonds of brotherly love. In other words, just as the New Testament is a charter enjoining Christian communities to live in peace with one another, so the Book of Tages containing the Etruscan Discipline enjoined the members of the federation to live in that manner. In practice the book actually enabled them to avoid the internecine wars which plagued pagan Greece and Italy and, later, Christian Europe.

What, then, did this Etruscan bible contain? First, it gave detailed instructions for divining the will of the gods, which was the equivalent of predicting the future. Since everything that had happened or was to happen had been decreed by the shrouded gods, the greatest importance was attached to precise and scientific methods of reading the omens. One method as laid down in the Book of Tages was divination by examination of the liver of a sacrificial sheep. Hepatoscopy is, perhaps, the most curious of all the many forms of fortune telling, and it tells us a great deal about the mentality and possibly the origin of the Etruscans; for the reading of omens in the entrails of animals was certainly a Babylonian contribution to the art of divination. Cicero, therefore, is correct in classing the Etruscans with the Chaldaeans as masters of this form of magic, though whether he and his compeers could witness the spectacle of a priest dabbling about in the guts of a dead animal as a convincing procedure for foretelling the future is doubtful. Yet the Romans did accept all forms of haruspicy as legitimate theological exercises, though they left the practice of liver-gazing to Etruscan priests who had long specialized in it.

We get some idea of what hepatoscopy involved by examining the famous bronze model of a liver found at Piacenza, since this object was evidently a demonstration model used to initiate novice priests into the mysteries of divination. A great deal of what appears to be plain wizardry now becomes more comprehensible. Indeed, it becomes clear that the priests were not relying on intuition as they examined the entrails of the sacrificial animal, but on specific formulas which were almost mathematical in conception. For the liver was divided into four quarters and each of these quarters into four, each section having its meaning

Mirror engraved with the figure of a haruspex in the act of examining the liver. He has been given the name of Calchas, the diviner who accompanied the Greek army to Troy.

145

in terms of a well thought out cosmography. In short, the haruspex was not examining a piece of flesh as he held the liver in the palm of one hand and felt its conformation with the fingers of the other; he was examining a microcosm of the universe.

The theory and practice of Etruscan divination, including hepatoscopy, could be said to have had a quite rational origin. That origin probably goes back to prehistoric times, to the last Ice Age when our European ancestors were particularly conscious of the relationship of the sun's position in the sky to the climate and length of day and of the benefits derived from its life-giving rays. If the Paleolithic inhabitant of the northern zone faced south in winter, he knew that in that direction lay the warm and benignant regions of the planet. Behind him to the north lay an enormous *terra incognita* covered in snow and ice. The southern sector of the sky, therefore, was the home of a kindly nature and, *ipso facto*, of the auspicious gods. And continuing the pattern we see that the east from the viewpoint of primitive man was the zone of the rising sun which brought light and warmth; the west, conversely, was the region of night and darkness and cold. Hence south and east were propitious and the seats of the divinities or nature-spirits friendly to man; north and west were inauspicious and belonged to the gods of darkness. Gradually men assigned specific gods to the celestial zones, the kindest gods to the south-east, the unfriendliest to the north-west. Thus, for each of the sixteen sectors into which the cosmos – and in Etruscan hepatoscopy, the liver – was divided, the name and seat of a deity were designated by long tradition; and what went on in the heavens (lightning flashes, thunder claps, shooting stars) and in animal organs (imperfections in the liver) were interpreted accordingly.

Beyond these general conjectures it is difficult if not impossible to go, though an immense amount of research has been done on the Piacenza bronze liver by leading German and French Etruscologists. Great progress was made in understanding this curious artefact after Professor Auguste Bouche-Leclercq drew attention in 1899 to the encyclopedia of Martianus Mineus Felix Capella and the relevance of this fourth-century compendium to the Etruscan system of divination. Martianus Capella was, like his more famous contemporary Augustine, a Romanized North African and resident of Carthage where around A.D. 400 he wrote a series of treatises on grammar, dialectics, oratory, rhetoric, geometry, arithmetic, astrology, and music. In one of these books, *De nuptiis Philologiae et Mercurii*, Capella obviously used sources based on the Etruscan Discipline. He lists sixteen compartments of the heavens and the gods who reside therein, beginning with those favourable to mankind and ending with those unfavourable. Professor Bouche-Leclercq's brilliant suggestion was that the sixteen regions or houses of Capella corresponded to the sixteen divisions of the Etruscan bronze liver. If the Professor's theory were correct, we would not only known the Latin equivalent of the Etruscan divine names, but how these

Bronze model of a liver divided into zones, each w the name of a god engrave upon it. The student pries used it to learn to divine t omens.

deities influenced for good or ill the course of human affairs. In other words, we would be on the verge of being able to practise divination in the Etruscan mode.

Beginning with the sixteen deities of the Etruscan pantheon as they are in-scribed in the sixteen segments round the edge of the Piacenza bronze liver and aided by Capella's list, we can at least make a start in identifying the principal Etruscan gods: for example Tinia (abbreviated to Tin) occupies the first three regions in the upper or north-eastern quadrant of the celestial vault, and this name must correspond to Capella's Jove who also resides in these three regions. The fourth region, or seat, is occupied by the Etruscan Ani Thne, and by the Latin Mulciber, a surname of Vulcan. They are probably, therefore, the same god. The eighth region has, on the Piacenza liver, the name Cetha; Capella calls it the Sun. The twelfth and thirteenth segments are occupied by Letham, corresponding to the Fates; the sixteenth and last, belongs to Vetisl, or Nocturnus, the god of Night.

From these clues we can deduce the four cardinal points which dominated Etruscan divination as follows:

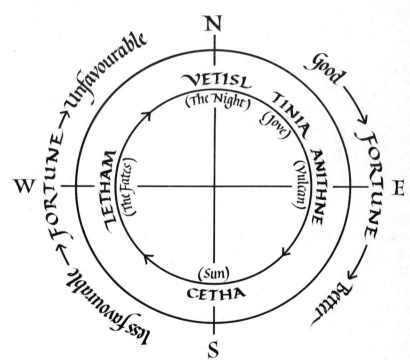

The theory of this Etruscan system of cosmic divination was based on the premise that there is no such thing as pure chance or coincidence: everything that befalls one must be the result of laws that govern the universe, not merely of physical laws, but also of spiritual forces. The fact that one of two men standing beneath a tree was struck by lightning while his companion remained unharmed was not coincidence to the Etruscans, but the operation of a supranatural law, 147 just as the fact that one of two men thrown into the sea survives because he can swim while the other drowns because he cannot is explicable by purely physical laws. For the essence of a truly pagan religion is that the gods order and control all activities of the universe: hence fate, destiny, fortune, or what we call chance is a reality as predictable as natural phenomena, like the flooding and ebbing of the tides. The Etruscan cosmology is very subtly summed up by Seneca in this comment: 'They believe not that things have significance because they have occurred, but that they have occurred because they have significance.'[1]

Conceiving of the laws of cause and effect in this manner, the Etruscans proceeded to examine the signals which came to them from many sources according to a carefully worked out system of divination. The evidence, if not the meaning, of the signals was all around for those who had eyes to see and ears to hear. It was conveyed in the direction of lightning flashes, claps of thunder, flights of birds, and the malformations in the organs of what should have been perfectly normal animals. All these phenomena occurred because they had significance. The augur's task was to discover the significance.

All primitive peoples, of course, are sensitive to obvious natural phenomena like thunder and lightning, drought and floods, earthquakes, dangerous animals, springs of water both hot and cold, and the mystery of trees. They read the signs given by these phenomena as we read the signs given us by our mechanical measuring devices. An obvious example is the restlessness of animals before a thunderstorm – behaviour which a primitive man can measure as effectively as modern man measures the behaviour of a column of mercury. So, to the pagan the whole of nature, in all its forms and activities, was linked together: gods, men, brute beasts, forests, fields, seas, and deserts – all were interdependent and what affected one part affected the whole, as a stone dropped in a pool was felt by every drop of water in that pool.

Haruspicy, or the inspection of entrails, was, then, part of this cosmic view; and since the Etruscans regarded the liver as the command post of the body, they were particularly interested in its condition. They were interested, as we have seen, because it was regarded as a microcosm of the entire universe, divided like the world into sixteen sections, each of which was the province of a particular god, exactly as each section of the sky was the seat of the same divinity. Knowing the location and the attributes of the god. the Etruscan priest was able to interpret the signs according to his Discipline, or to the science which had been handed down to him through the ages in the Book of Tages. And though this book is lost, along with everything the Etruscans wrote apart from funerary inscriptions, a number of hand mirrors depict for us the ritual of liver-gazing. In the engravings on the backs of these mirrors we see how the liver of the sacrificial animal was held in the palm of the diviner's left hand with the two large lobes allowed to hang down like pouches. The fingers of the right hand then slid over the surface of the liver, feeling for imperfections in the various sectors assigned to

Statuette of a girl. An example of Etruscan plastic art in which the same Ionian influence is evident as in the famous Apollo of Veii (see page 151).

[1] Lucius Annaeus Seneca, *Naturales Quaestiones*, II, 32, 2.

A haruspex, or Etruscan priest, whose function it was to interpret the omens, particularly as found in the livers of sheep.

particular gods. A defect in the north-western area of the gland would be interpreted as a sinister omen, while a formation of some sort in the south-eastern region, seat of the favourable gods, would indicate good fortune. The portraits of the diviner at work on the back of the so-called Tarchon mirror found in a tomb at Tuscania (Toscanella) shows the priest with the liver in his left hand which rests on his left knee, his left foot being placed on a boulder, no doubt a sacred stone, possibly a meteorite. The right foot of the diviner is placed at right angles to the left foot, with the sole set flat on the ground and, since we find this stance reproduced in other portraits of haruspices, we can be sure that such was the ritual posture of the liver-gazers. The costume, too, was canonically decreed: a hat shaped like a cone with ribbons hanging from the brim was tied under the chin, a necessary precaution as the divination appears to have been carried out in the open air, perhaps in a grove sanctified for the purpose. In addition to his ecclesiastical hat, the priest wore a pleated cloak fastened at the breast by a clasp of the safety-pin type and under the cloak a short tunic closed at the neck. Evidently haruspicy was carried out early in the morning because the slanting rays of the sun would reveal blemishes more clearly at that time of day; and judging from the number of divinities assigned a position on the bronze model found at Piacenza, the diviner would need highly sensitive fingers and sharp eyes, for he had a total of some forty deities to choose from, five of them grouped inside the gall bladder alone, with another nine placed around this area.

Equally important for interpreting the will and the word of the gods were the direction and volume of thunder claps, the special means of communication between heaven and earth and hence the voice of the gods themselves. The Etruscans had refined the primitive animistic fears of thunder into a comprehensible system, though where they derived their theory from is completely unknown. However, according to them, nine gods had the right to hurl thunderbolts, of which there were eleven sorts; and the rules for interpreting the direction, duration, and attendant lightning flashes of these bolts were laid down in the second volume of the Etruscan bible – what the Romans referred to as the *libri fulgurales*. These books, like those concerned with liver inspection (*libri haruspicini*), have disappeared completely, though the Romans were quite familiar with them and incorporated them into their own native system of divination; so it is from references in Roman literature that we learn that the chief god Tinia (Jupiter) hurls three; his wife Uni (Juno) hurls her bolts; Menvra (Minerva) hurls hers; Cilens (Summanus, the guardian of the gates) hurls his by night; Sethlans (Vulcan) hurls his; so does Maris (Mars) and several other 'thunderers'. These gods were favourable or ill-disposed towards mankind according to the place they occupied in the heavens: hence it was important for the priest responsible for divining celestial phenomena like thunder, lightning, and shooting stars to observe first where the activity originated; second, where it ended; and third, which direction it took in its passage from heaven to earth.

In general, if the signs came down from the priest's left (which was the east as the fulguriator faced south for the divination ceremony), the omens were good, as the east was the seat of the beneficent deities; if the sign came from the right (or west) the auspices were unfavourable for the converse reason. And so the priest's task was threefold: to observe, to interpret, and to recommend correct procedure for placating the gods. If the auspices had been favourable, the worshipper was required to abase himself in gratitude; and if they were unfavourable, to abase himself in the hope of mercy.

A religious creed as god-fearing as that of the Etruscans was bound to foster a slave mentality – a state of mind which appealed to neither the Greeks nor the Romans, though the latter people, in their formative period at any rate, were deeply impressed by the pseudo-science of Etruscan divination. Later on, as the Romans turned away from the ancient superstitions and absorbed the Greek life-enhancing philosophy, they came to regard the Etruscan Discipline as a sort of anthropological curiosity, as Europeans regard African witchcraft. And the reason for this is largely the refusal of a successful and highly materialistic people to accept the cardinal principle of all pagan theology: namely, the utter helplessness of mere man in his relationship with the gods.

It has been observed that the religion of a people can be gauged by the place of Hell in their system. The Etruscan Hell is as dreadful a place as the Inferno of the Middle Ages which, in fact, it somewhat resembles, what with its hideous fiery-eyed demons and terrible lords of the underworld. The king of these nether regions was Mantus, but the two infernal figures most characteristic of Etruscan demonology are Charun and Tuchulcha, for this hideous pair seem to be the prototypes of all the devils of the early Christian Hell, embodying the terrors which afflict, or are supposed to afflict, the wicked. Charun is not the benign old ferryman of Greek legend; he is a fearsome monster with the head of a wolf on the body of a man and he invariably carries as the badge of his office a large hammer with which he crushes the skulls of the dying in order to finish them off. As if this were not enough to remind living Etruscans of the terrors of death, Charun has a comrade in the person of Tuchulcha, a monster calculated to give nightmares to the most righteous of mortals. Whereas Charun has the flaming eyes and fangs of a wolf, Tuchulcha has the face of a vulture with the ears of a donkey and the snake-infested hair of a harpy. What his functions were is not clear, since it is assumed that by the time the newly deceased had been battered by Charun, there would be no point in Tuchulcha frightening him to death with his terrifying beak, wings, and serpents. But he is shown in a mural of a Tarquinian tomb as doing precisely this to Theseus and Pirithous on their expedition down to Hades in an attempt to rescue Persephone.

Significantly the Etruscan devils make their appearance relatively late in history, about half way through the fourth century B.C., in fact, when the power and prestige of the Confederation were in decline. Moreover, the later the date,

The Apollo of Veii. Detail of the head and shoulders of a terracotta statue, recognized as a masterpiece of Ionian-Etruscan art. It portrays the god, whose name originally meant 'Destroyer', as the ideal of manly youth and beauty.

the more horrendous the portraits of the devils, which suggests that the religious beliefs of the Etruscans became sterner as the Twelve Cities lost their importance and succumbed one by one to the Romans. And so the threat of terrible punishments for the wicked was introduced, while the pleasant banquets we see taking place in the tombs may symbolize the reward for heroes. Certainly we conclude from the religious literature of the Babylonians, the Jews, and other oriental peoples that the priests invariably ascribed the national woes – defeats on the battlefield, droughts, plagues, and so forth – to the wickedness of the people, wickedness which had to be punished by somebody somewhere, hence the necessity of devils and hells of one sort or another.

But in a sense these late importations into the Etruscan theology were irrelevant, since the religion had always been based on the irrevocable decrees of fate. Against this fate, which the Etruscans conceived as so powerful that it controlled even the gods, it was useless for man to struggle, to alter his life, or to try and influence the course of events. If fate had decreed that he was to be a king or a slave, happy or miserable, longlived or cut off in his prime, there was nothing he could do to change it. Yes, there was just one thing, one small option left to the individual: his only hope of appeasing the jealous gods was to be humble and contrite, to abase himself, either to give thanks or to plead for mercy. It was just possible, if the gods could be bribed by a royal enough gift, that some postponement of evil fortune might be arranged for, though postponement only, for nothing, no prayers, no sacrifices, no expiations could alter the inevitable or delay indefinitely the decrees of the shrouded gods.

It is evident that religion of this variety has none of the moral imperatives of later cults which offer all men the hope of salvation and the rewards of heaven in return for conformity to particular tenets laid down by the founder of the cult. The Etruscan religion had no founder, and it had no moral tenets such as 'thou shalt not kill', 'thou shalt not commit adultery', or 'thou shalt love thy neighbour as thyself'. To the Etruscans, and to all pagans, for that matter, such commandments were impracticable and had nothing to do with religion. In any case, the gods themselves did not practise them. Even so, the Discipline dominated and controlled the lives of Etruscans, but, unluckily for them, not as a lifegiving but as a deadening force. For it is certain that in the intellectual climate induced by this stultifying fatalism, there was little incentive for men to explore the universe in a spirit of scientific objectivity, to discuss philosophical or ethical problems, or to alter the structure of society. They seem to have sought their happiness through the indulgence of their senses, or so they appear to depict themselves in those strange and beautiful portraits they left behind, characteristically, in their tombs. On the evidence of these pictures alone it would be quite wrong to think of them as a gloomy and despairing people because their religion was gloomy and despairing. On the contrary, they went banqueting and dancing and playing their flutes to the underworld itself.

Tomb of the Augurs, Tarquinia, 6th century B.C. A priest is evidently releasing a bird in order to divine the omens. The other walls of this tomb are painted with scenes depicting games played in honour of the deceased.

CHAPTER NINE

Literature, Art, and Science

THE GREATEST of the Roman encyclopedists, Marcus Terentius Varro (116–27 B.C.), tells us that he used Etruscan texts in the compilation of his four hundred and ninety books, which covered nearly every field of science and art. Varro was born at Reate (today Rieti) in the country of the Sabines, so he may actually have heard Etruscan being spoken, since the language had not at that time died out and was, indeed, to linger on as a country dialect for another three or four centuries. Be that as it may, Varro certainly consulted annals written by Etruscan historians for his principal work, *The Divine Antiquities*, which treats of the history, geography, and anthropology of pre-Augustan Italy. This treatise is now regrettably lost, though from the frequent references made to it by other classical writers, it was a source of political, social, and religious history which can never be replaced, particularly with respect to the Etruscans. What is so vexing to modern students of ancient Italian history is that the *Antiquities* was apparently still extant in A.D. 1320 when the poet Petrarch actually saw them, for he wrote that he searched eagerly for them in later life without success. The likeliest explanation of the sudden disappearance of the book seems to be its deliberate suppression by the Church on the grounds that it was nothing but a collection of blasphemous superstitions and that it detracted from the glory of St Augustine's *City of God*, a work which is obviously greatly indebted to Varro's *Divine Antiquities*.

With the disappearance of this irreplaceable book, our chances of ever knowing what the Etruscans achieved in the field of literature became remote. We can only accept as true the statements of Varro, Polybius, Dionysius of Halicarnassus, Lucretius, and others that they did possess a national literature and that their books included histories, dramas, poems, and didactic texts of one sort or another. The proof of their literacy is seen in the numerous representations of men, women, and children holding open scrolls or tablets. Unfortunately, not a vestige of their writings has come down to us, with the exception of a few hundred lines of what are obviously religious and ritual texts; and this absence has led some commentators to doubt whether there ever was an Etruscan literary tradition at all. It has been argued that inasmuch as Etruscan society was a rigid theocracy, Etruria, like Sumer, Babylonia, Egypt, and the other oriental theocracies, produced very little secular literature. Thus,

Detail from an Attic vase found in Etruria showing the Greek concept of Apollo, seen here in the presence of Zeus.

Villanovan cinerary urn in the shape of a wattle and daub hut. 8th century B.C.

the histories, dramas, and poems which the Roman writers refer to are assumed to be religious annals, mystery plays, and hymns, comparable perhaps with the church literature of the Middle Ages. Certainly a number of the ritualistic writings of the Etruscans – notably those books dealing with divination – were incorporated into the Roman scriptures, rather as the chronicles of the Jews have been incorporated into the Christian Bible. Nothing else has survived, for the obvious reason that after the fifth century A.D. there was no longer anybody left who could read the language or any scribe who could copy what books did remain on the shelves of a few private libraries.

As for their literature, so for the music which was such an integral part of their lives that it was always played at religious festivals, banquets, athletic contests, and featured in their tomb paintings. We shall never know what songs the Etruscans sang, or what melodies they played on their pipes and trumpets. But it is certain that their music was highly sophisticated, for they developed a whole variety of orchestral instruments. The strings included the zither and the lyre; the wind instruments the double pipes and the trumpet; the percussion instruments, the castanets which were used by ballerinas who danced with the same gestures we see in Spanish flamenco dancing today.

Music, then, accompanied almost every religious and social activity, so much

so that it seems the Etruscans were unable to stage a wrestling match without a melody on the pipes. It was probably this passion for music which excited the scorn of the stern Roman moralists who equated the 'soft Lydian airs' with depravity. In the good old days, the Romans restricted music to the battlefield and other martial occasions, the trumpet with its loud masculine tone being their approved instrument.

Obviously we shall never know the Etruscans through either their literature or their music, both of which arts tell us so much about the thoughts and emotions of a nation. In this respect our loss is irreparable, for we are left with very few other sources of information concerning their private lives. True, the experts can reconstruct from the scenes sculpted on the sepulchral urns what their public buildings and even their houses looked like, and we can pick up odds and ends of information on the latter from classical historians who mention certain architectural details like porticos and interior courtyards with central water tanks, familiar to us from the remains found all over Europe of Roman villas whose foundations have survived. We know, too, that the Etruscans were thoroughgoing town planners, for they regarded their cities not merely as convenient centres for commerce, but as sacred places in the service of the gods as well as of men. Because of this, the site for a settlement was carefully selected

Detail from a painting in the Tomb of the Augurs, Tarquinia. Two wrestlers are accompanied by an augur who watches the flight of the birds.

and before the ground was broken an augur took the omens; only if these were auspicious did the king or chieftain cut the furrow which marked the city limits. To do this according to the ancient rite, he took up his position behind a white cow and a white bull yoked together to a plough, the bull on the outside. The plough was the symbolic instrument that traced the furrow that was to sanctify the city limits for all time; and so that there should be no mistake, the followers of the plough turned the sod inwards towards the city, thus marking the line of the walls, while the furrow marked the line of the fosse, or outer ditch. Upon reaching the site of a gate, the plough was lifted from the ground, since this stretch of the city boundary was deliberately left unsanctified in order, says Plutarch, that necessary but unclean goods could be sent in and taken out by way of the gates. We are not told what goods were considered unclean, but we know from Jewish ritual how strict was religious law in these matters. The extreme care with which the Etruscan rites were observed is further illustrated in the convention of leaving the city gates unconsecrated, whereas the walls were dedicated to the gods who, it was hoped, would protect the citizens inside them from their enemies. One further ceremony was involved – the designation of a strip of land inside the walls to be left for ever as a sort of green belt or park where no houses were to be built. Finally the tracks of the north–south *cardo* and the east–west *decumanus* were surveyed and the point where they intersected designated the gateway to the next world. In this way the Etruscans placed their cities under the protection of the gods and planned them for the benefit of the citizens.

Once the priests had fulfilled their function of laying a city's foundations according to religious law, the architects and civil engineers took over the job

Etruscan bronze work of an early rustic type, depicting a farm scene with a plough-man and his team.

of making the place safe, clean, and comfortable. Particular attention was paid to drainage and sewerage. For, as their tens of thousands of rock tombs demonstrate, the Etruscans were especially skilled at tunnelling and subterranean excavations. They put these skills to the service of the living in boring tunnels which diverted the courses of rivers or drained lakes in order to reclaim land they needed for agriculture. All these engineering techniques were later learned by the Romans, judging from what survives of their early sewerage system. The *cloaca maxima*, which carried the wastes of north-east Rome down to the Tiber by way of a brick tunnel, is still said to be serviceable in places.

Inside their houses, furniture and furnishings were simple compared with the variety and quantity of objects in the modern home. The reason is self-evident, since it still obtains to some extent in the small towns and villages throughout the Mediterranean lands: people seek their entertainment in the streets and regard their houses as mere shelters in which to eat and sleep. In Etruria, the stone-built and timber-roofed buildings were invariably public edifices – temples to the gods, palaces of the kings, and courts of law. The ordinary citizens were content with humbler dwellings, though as the merchants and tradesmen prospered, they no doubt built better houses for themselves and furnished them more luxuriously. The extent of that prosperity is revealed by

Sketch by George Dennis of an Etruscan *cloaca* or sewer at Marta near Bolsena. The Etruscans introduced the arch to the early Romans.

the incalculable amount of treasure taken out of the tombs during the nineteenth century, which we should remember is only a fraction of what these burial chambers once contained, seeing that they had been looted in previous centuries by barbarian invaders from the north. The old tomb robbers, however, were not interested in the urns and little stone chests containing the ashes of the dead Etruscans, so they left these articles *in situ*, though a number of the sarcophagi have had the lids pried off just to make sure that there were no golden ornaments on the corpse. If there were such ornaments, of course, the robbers purloined them. Vases appear to have been of no particular value to these early looters and, provided such vases were empty, they were left on the benches where they had been placed by the relatives of the deceased. Usually, however, they were found by later excavators scattered all over the burial chamber, indicating that the robbers were in a hurry and so knocked them out of the way in order to get at some other article of more immediate value. These treasure seekers were, of course, after gold, jewels, armour, and weapons.

Despite the indiscriminate plundering of the Etruscan cemeteries during the

Small votive bronze of an Etruscan ploughman with his team of yoked oxen, a sight that is still occasionally seen in rural Tuscany. 4th century B.C.

Dark Ages, the quantity of vases found in mint condition by modern excavators is quite incredible, as any visitor to the principal Etruscan collections knows from a casual stroll through the galleries. Many of these vases are, of course, of Greek provenance, while the majority, even when manufactured in Etruria by Etruscan potters, are decorated with Greek mythological themes. One can hardly say that they tell us much about the people who owned them, except that the Etruscans themselves were prosperous enough in their heyday to import the finest products of foreign workshops.

Bronze mirrors, on the other hand, are more revealing of Etruscan taste, since they represent the intimate and personal possessions of identifiable individuals – women whose names are sometimes inscribed on the mirror itself or over the portal of the tomb in which the article was found. We know of some one thousand five hundred examples of these hand mirrors, dating from the sixth to the third century B.C. They are especially valuable to both the social and the art historian, for they tell us, if only by implication, something about the private side of Etruscan society, which is the area of our greatest ignorance.

Apparently the circular bronze mirror, highly polished on one side and engraved with a picture story on the back, is an Etruscan invention, for no such mirrors have come down to us from Greece. This is not altogether surprising if we remember the lowly status of Greek women and, conversely, the respect accorded to Etruscan matrons. In other words, the latter were indulged in their wishes, the proof of which is not only the extraordinary number of beautiful mirrors that have survived but the quantity and, above all, the quality of their jewellery – coronets, rings, and necklaces the design and workmanship of which are the quintessence of elegance. Mirrors, on the other hand, appear to have been romantic as well as practical possessions, for the purpose of the engraving on the back was evidently to entertain a lady while she performed her toilet. And so the objects must be representative of the Etruscan woman's taste in art and literature. In particular there seems to be a natural preference for love stories involving brave men and fair women: hence, the prevalence of courting scenes between the more handsome of the heroes and the more beautiful of the heroines – Aphrodite, Helen, Adonis, and Paris. Nor are the husbands and children forgotten in the picture book on the back of the lady's mirror, for there are a great many depicting adventure stories condensed, of course, into a single scene. But invariably the characters of the drama are beautiful to look at, the men young, slim, and athletic; the women rosy and rounded in limb – both sexes naked and completely devoid of lubricity. The contrast between the Greco-Etruscan presentation of the naked body and that of the modern commercialized pin-up tells us more about the difference in the two cultures than any number of books. We see this in a scene in which the maiden Atalanta is shown wrestling with a male athlete in honour of King Pelias, whose principal distinction, according to the official biographers, seems to have been siring an enormous

TOP Kylix, or wine cup, from Vulci, depicting wrestlers, one being tossed in the 'flying mare' throw, permitted in the Greek Olympic games, but now classed as a foul.

BOTTOM Panathenaic amphora from Vulci, about 490 B.C. Greek vases, like this one by the Eucharides painter illustrating a horse race, were given as prizes to winners of athletic contests.

OVERLEAF Banquet scene in the Tomb of the Leopards, Tarquinia, mid-5th century B.C. This tomb, named after the pair of splendid beasts featured above the semi-reclining diners, reveals by its scenes of revelry both the pleasures of life on earth and the expectations of life in the hereafter.

number of daughters who later cut him up and boiled him in order to restore his youth and vigour. It is not known whether this experiment was successful, only that Pelias was honoured at the Olympic games, which is why Atalanta, an athlete of Olympian standards, was wrestling. But there was nothing brutal or distasteful in her encounter, since the graceful girl, so neat in her elegant cap and close-fitting shorts, easily threw her opponent – to the delight, no doubt, of the Etruscan ladies who told their daughters the story as they examined their faces in the mirror.

And how evocative is the engraving showing the reconciliation, at the insistence of Aphrodite, of Helen and Paris! Aphrodite is shown grasping the chin of the beautiful Mycenean queen who tries to push the goddess's hand away. Paris gazes longingly at his mistress. Etruscan women of a romantic or sentimental nature must have loved to look at this scene and to hear again the wonderful story of Helen and Paris and the siege of Troy; or, gazing at the back of another mirror showing Jason being cared for by Medea and Minerva, to dream, perhaps of how they had once nursed their own absent husbands or sons. These mirrors must in some cases have become very dear to the women who used them, for we find examples which were inscribed with the owner's name and hence buried with her at her request. A beautiful mirror found in a tomb at Perugia is interesting in this respect, for it carries along the floral border the words *Ceithurneal Sutheria*, which is translated as 'The tomb property of Ceithurnei'. We can assume that this lady had sons only, for otherwise a mirror was bound to be passed on to a daughter.

As for Etruscan vases, they, too, can be studied and enjoyed from various viewpoints. Many of them are beautiful just to look at, without complicating one's aesthetic pleasure by problems as to their provenance, age, and style. Others are interesting to specialists in the history of ceramics, which is so integral a part of the history of early western culture. Others, again, reflect the changes in historical periods almost as precisely as official annals – if such had been kept and preserved. In addition, the vessels designed for holding wine, water, oil, or unguents also served as picture books for the Etruscan family, to the extent that the illustrations glazed round their bowls told the familiar stories of the age. Just as the heroes of popular entertainment today are often supermen, whether cowboys, detectives, or spies, so to the Etruscans they were the gods whose adventures provided the vase painters with themes for their story telling, as they provided plots for the dramatists and poets. Probably this is why Hercules, the champion of mortals against the ineluctable gods, appears so frequently on Etruscan vases, followed in popularity by those divinities who seem to reveal certain human traits – Aphrodite in her sexuality, Dionysus in his excesses, Apollo in his love of the arts. So Hercules was the personification of the super-man, eternally fascinating since he was the son of Zeus and an earthly mother, not, however, by immaculate conception which would have made him wholly

Gold wine cup from the Bernardini tomb, Palestrina. The 7th-century B.C. Etruscan goldsmith has added sphinxes as handles to a Corinthian design.

165

divine, but by the usual natural process. Thus, during the absence of her husband Amphitryon on business, his mother Alcmene was visited by Zeus in the form of her earthly spouse. Her son was the result of the god's nocturnal visit, which lasted one night in earthly time but was prolonged into three nights by celestial time. The story of the god's desire for a mortal woman, as well as the deceitful manner in which he obtained her favours, at the same time deliberately cuckold-ing her husband (a crime punishable by death among mortals), demonstrated that the gods took what they wanted when and how they wanted it, even at the expense of the innocent. It is no wonder, therefore, that a hero like Hercules, who was prepared to challenge the gods, was the most popular of all the pagan divinities and that generations of his admirers never tired of hearing how he struck a blow for men against tyrants, whether divine or human. Even as an infant he was the champion of mortals, for he outwitted his implacable enemy, Hera, the queen of heaven, who sent snakes to kill the baby son of her husband's mistress in his cradle; and the baby promptly wrung their necks. Again, the queen-goddess was outwitted when, on the occasion of one of those curious pranks the gods used to indulge in, Hermes, the practical joker, carried the infant Hercules up to Olympus and attached him to Hera's breast while she was asleep. But waking, she shoved the hated infant aside, spilling her milk which thus produced the Milky Way.

And so the exploits of Hercules depicted on various household utensils provided the themes for a number of oft-told adventure stories, just as the trophy vases celebrating the victories of athletes in the public games reminded the Etruscans of the achievements of mortal heroes. The sheer number of these vases illustrating the contests of legendary or actual supermen reveals the Etruscan passion for sport which, like all other public activities, was religious in origin and purpose. There can hardly be any other explanation of those tomb paintings which picture wrestling, boxing, and gladiatorial combats, for very early in pagan history all forms of sport had been organized into religious festivals – the Olympic games being dedicated to Zeus, the Panathenaea to Athena. Both festivals were sanctified with sacrifices, prayers, and religious processions, after which the contests were held in honour of god and country. The Etruscans for their part either brought their own type of festival with them from their Lydian homeland, or had imitated the Greek institutions; and in due course they passed on their passion for games to the Romans. Indeed, some scholars argue that the Etruscans were not only responsible for teaching the Romans the sports of the arena but also for the spirit of blood lust which characterized the Roman gladia-torial shows. According to this view, the carnage in the imperial amphitheatres originated with the Etruscan custom of sacrificing prisoners of war at ceremonies in honour of their own dead; and as evidence of this the apologists for the Romans refer to the slaughter of three hundred and seven Roman captives in the forum of Tarquinia in 358 B.C. This primitive method of disposing of prisoners,

Blindfolded man being baited by a dog. An example of the Etruscan gladiatorial-type combats which the Romans later adopted. The painting is from the Tomb of the Augurs, Tarquinia, 530 B.C.

it is said, led to the more sophisticated form of murder whereby prisoners were forced to fight to the death in the arena – in other words to present a gladiatorial combat for the entertainment of the crowd. Proof that the Etruscans did encourage such combats, however, depends to some extent on how one interprets the evidence. There are, for instance, a number of tomb paintings from Tarquinia showing contests between armed men. One such painting shows a fight between a man with a dog and a man armed with a club – the armed gladiator apparently being blindfolded. He seems to have been badly bitten by the ferocious hound. Other pictures are said by some to foreshadow the Roman wild beast hunts in which hundreds of animals imported from all over the empire were goaded into killing each other in the arena, or were slaughtered by specially trained hunters called *bestiarii*. In addition, several cinerary urns in the Guarnacci Museum in Volterra depict scenes of bull-fighting, horse racing, and gladiatorial combats. From this sort of evidence and the specific statements of the historians, we are bound to admit that the Romans received the idea of the circus from the Etruscans.

On the other hand, it is equally certain that the Romans soon ceased to associate sport with religion and staged their public games simply for the advancement of the sponsor and the gratification of the mob. It is also certain that what there had been of strength, grace, and dignity in the Greek athletics where, as at Olympia, the prizes consisted of chaplets of wild olive, was degraded 167

Frieze on an urn depicting a sacrifice to the accompaniment of orchestral music.

in the Roman arenas into such brutal and disgusting spectacles that before the games were abolished altogether, men and animals were being massacred in their thousands and women were being publicly violated in the ring.

But no such sadistic scenes are depicted on the Etruscan vases which commemorate athletic contests in the spirit of the primitive religious festivals. And if an amphora in the British Museum is typical, it sums up this simple, rather rustic approach of the Etruscans to sport. Nine scenes are portrayed. In the first, two boxers face each other in the stance still seen in old-fashioned prints of pugilists. They are boxing to the sound of the flute. The second scene shows a young man climbing what appears to be a greasy pole. The third depicts a pair of acrobats wrestling; the fourth, a discus and javelin thrower; the fifth, a race in full armour; the sixth, a chariot race; the seventh, male dancers; the eighth, female dancers; the ninth, boys dancing to the accompaniment of castanets.

There is one other aspect of Etruscan art which is of paramount importance. It is the practice of writing what appear to be captions to the actual illustrations on mirrors, vases, and tomb paintings. In such cases, the theory is that the picture will give us the meaning of the words and so provide much-needed evidence not only of the Etruscan orthography and vocabulary, but even of the grammar. An example of such a combination of picture and caption is found on a painted vase unearthed at Vulci. The vessel is a mixing bowl, possibly made in the fourth century B.C., and it shows the principal characters in the story of the Thessalian king Admetus and his wife Alcestis, written in Etruscan as Atmite and Alcsti. Admetus, it seems, had forgotten to sacrifice to Artemis, the goddess of the forest, and so was condemned to die unless someone would offer himself in his place. His wife Alcestis offered to make the necessary sacrifice. The Etruscan artist has chosen the moment when husband and wife meet for the last time before the victim is consigned to the underworld by two hideous demons, the well-known Charun with his hammer and the winged angel of death with his serpents. One cannot claim that the Etruscan artist has done justice to this drama, for his portraits of the two principals are stiff and uninspired, and he seems to have had more feeling for the gruesome Charun and his companion demon than for the beautiful and loving Alcestis of the legend. However, the caption which belongs with this scene and which reads in Etruscan

ECA : ERSCE : NAC : ACHRUM : PHLERTHRCE

can be loosely translated as:

The farewell of Admetus and Alcestis, with Charun wielding his hammer and the angel of death holding his serpents. From an Etruscan vase found at Vulci.

Lo! She embraces her husband and offers
herself as a sacrifice to the Underworld

which, it should be added, is one of various literal translations of the text, indicating how controversial the Etruscan language is and why it is the most difficult area of all Etruscan studies.

CHAPTER TEN

Language

THERE ARE over nine thousand inscriptions in Etruscan, and almost all of them can be understood without much difficulty. It seems strange, therefore, to speak of Etruscan as an unknown language, particularly when we have no special problems in reading an inscription like this one – the replica of an inscription from the Tomb of the Tryphon at Tarquinia – presenting at first appearance a completely unrecognizable script:

Ǝꓱ ΛꓶƎ᠈ ᴎΑꓶ᠈ ꓶΑꝊᴎΑ᠈ ᛃ∇ꓶᴡ∇ꓶ᠈ ᛃꝹΑꓶᛃꓱ

The explanation is simple.[1] First, the letters are obviously derived from an archaic Greek alphabet, some of them (the A and I, for instance) being easily recognizable. Indeed, scholars as early as the eighteenth century worked out the values of most of the Etruscan characters and, once they had perceived that the writing was to be read from right to left, they had no difficulty in deciphering the names of gods and heroes like Aplu for the Greek Apollo, Hercle for Hercules or Herakles, and Aleχsantre for Alexander. Gradually the whole alphabet, with the phonetic values of the individual letters, was established, so that anyone can, with the aid of a table (see opposite), read an Etruscan inscription and often recognize an Etruscan name.

Unfortunately the identification of the alphabet and even the fact of being able to read and pronounce the words does not adduce the sense of them; and it was only thanks to the discovery of a few bilingual texts that the philologists were able to get a glimpse of the Etruscan vocabulary and grammar. Thus, the inscription on the marble urn given below happens to have a Latin translation on the reverse of the vessel, as follows:

ꓶΑΙꓘΑ ᗺΑꓶ ᠈ ᗞ∀ꟻ∀Iꟼꟻ ᠈ ꓘ∇ꓶ

P. VOLUMNIUS CAFATIA NATUS

Now, reading the words from right to left, we can transliterate the Etruscan inscription as:

PUP. VELIMNA. CAHATIAL

and translate it with the aid of the Latin gloss as:

P(UBLIUS) VOLUMNIUS SON OF CAHATIA

[1] LARIS. PUMPUS. ARNTHAL. CLAN. CECHASE. In English, Lars Pompey, son of Arnth. The last word is probably a verb, but its meaning is not known.

Etruscan	A	𐌁	𐌂	𐌃	𐌄	𐌅	I	𐌇	⊗	I	𐌊	𐌋	𐌌	𐌍
Greek	A	B	Γ	Δ	E	Ϝ	Z	(H)	Θ	I	K	Λ	M	N
English	A	B	C	D	E	V	Z	H	Th	I	K	L	M	N

Etruscan	⊞	O	𐌐	M	Q	𐌃	𐌔	T	Y	X	φ	↓	8 archaic
Greek		O	π			P	Σ	T	Y	X	φ		
English	(S)	O	P	Ś	Q	R	S	T	U	Ṡ	(Ph)	(Ch)	F

The letters of the Etruscan alphabet with their Greek and English equivalents.

And so this bilingual, together with some thirty other examples, enables us to translate practically all the other funerary inscriptions extant, since the great majority of them consist of a simple description of the name, parentage, and age of the deceased. Further, certain useful clues of a grammatical nature are provided by the translation of the Etruscan *Cahatial* into the Latin *Cafatia natus*, since this shows that the Etruscan genitive is formed by the suffix ⁓*al*. Other bilinguals tell us that the suffix ⁓*c* added to a word meant 'and', rather like the Latin *que* in the phrase *senatus populusque*.

A third source of our knowledge of Etruscan comes from the glosses scattered about the writings of Greek and Roman authors who discuss an occasional Etruscan word and give its Latin equivalent in their own language. Strabo, writing in the first century B.C., states that the Etruscan word for 'monkey' was *harimos* (ἁρίμος), though the word is not found in any extant Etruscan text. Verrius Flaccus, a freedman of the Age of Augustus and author of a book called *Libri Rerum Etruscarum*, now unfortunately lost along with all the other works of this learned man, states that the Latin admonition *arce ignem* ('beware of fire') was *arse verse* in Etruscan, which, however, looks suspect even on the face of it. The most useful (and trustworthy) of these glosses is that of the grammarian Hesychius of Alexandria who wrote in the fifth century A.D. He gives the meaning of 'gods' to the Etruscan word he spells in the Greek fashion *aisoi* (ἀισοί). This word appears frequently in the literature as *aisar* (plural) and *ais* (singular). It is found so regularly in the Book of the Mummy that the religious nature of this still untranslated document is certain.

If all that survived of Etruscan writing were inscriptions on tombstones, the non⁓specialist would have no interest in the language as such; but there are just enough other texts available in this ancient tongue to constitute a modest literature which scholars have been trying to translate since Giovanni Nanni of 171

Viterbo in 1498 claimed to have found the key in Aramaic. The material they have to work on, omitting for the present the funerary and votive inscriptions, consists of: first, the Book of the Mummy, containing a total of one thousand five hundred words, of which, however, only five hundred are different on account of the constant repetition of words and phrases; and second, about ten long or fairly long inscriptions of one sort or another on monuments, statues, tiles, tablets, and sarcophagi. From these sources we can compile a vocabulary of about a thousand Etruscan words.

We have, therefore, sufficient linguistic material to work on, and no doubt the difficulties of translating these texts would have been quickly overcome if only Etruscan could be related to some other family of languages. There has been no shortage of attempts to find the key and almost every conceivable language in the world has been tested for the purpose. A short list would include Hebrew, Aramaic, Greek, Latin, Hittite, Lydian, Coptic, Chaldaean, Egyptian, Celtic, Gothic, Rhaeto-Romansch, Albanian, Basque, Abhaz, Ubykh, Adaghe (with its two dialects Kabardi and Kiakh), Cheehen, Avaro-Andi, Samu, Lakk or Kasi-Kumuk, Artchi, Hinalugh, Iddi, Mingrebian, Svanetian, and Old Norse. Enthusiasts who have claimed to have found the key in one or the other of these languages always state their theory with complete conviction, proceed to translate the original texts on the basis of what they have assumed, and are immediately called fools or charlatans by their fellow Etruscologists. Within a short time their efforts are forgotten and still another theorist appears on the scene with still another translation. And so the same ground is gone over again and again; and the same languages are translated or tortured into some sort of relationship with the elusive Etruscan.

The earliest commentators automatically assumed that Hebrew was the mother tongue of all languages, since Adam and Eve were the progenitors of the human race and presumably spoke Hebrew, the language of Genesis. Later students like Luigi Lanzi suggested as early as 1789, though only cautiously, that Etruscan was closely related to either Greek or Latin. This theory, periodically restated from time to time, is perhaps the most popular of them all and has had the support of many erudite professors. None the less, it, too, is rejected.

Rejected also is the theory put forward by Professor Carl Schmitz who attempted to explain Etruscan in terms of German, as Sir William Betham had tried to do in terms of Old Irish. Robert Ellis, Fellow of St John's College, Cambridge, had no more success in 1861 with his theory of the Armenian origin of Etruscan. Canon Isaac Taylor came forward fifteen years later with the proposal that Etruscan belonged to the Turanian family of languages whence the key was to be found in 'Finnic, Turkic, Mongolic, Dravidic, and Malayic dialects.' By 1887 Adolfo Borromei had suggested still another source – Sanskrit. No sooner had the objections of the other philologists died down over

Tombstone of an Etruscan warrior called Avele Feluske. He is shown armed with a double-bladed axe. The inscription is in archaic Etruscan.

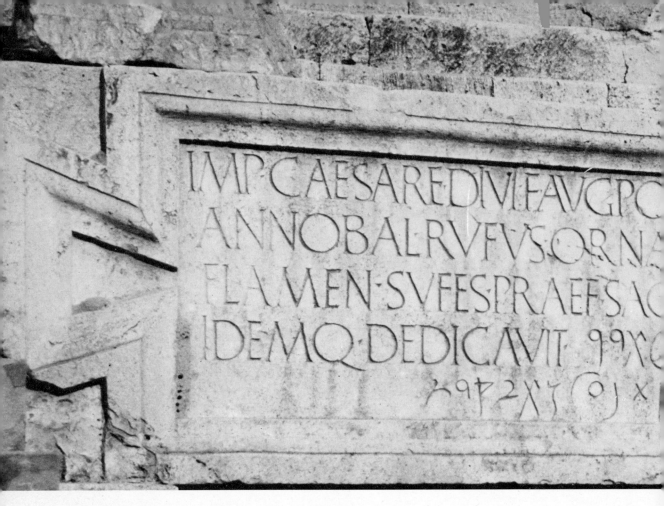

Borromei's novel theory than in 1889 the American anthropologist Daniel Garrison Brinton (who, as we have seen, claimed that the Red Indians migrated to the North American continent from Europe and not from Asia) argued that Etruscan was related to the Berber, Kabyle, and Tuareg languages of Africa. In 1911 Baron Bernard Carra de Vaux looked much further to the north for a related language and found the connection in the Urals. Jakobos Thomopoulos moved south again to Albania, Jules Martha north to Finland, Ernst Littman east to Lydia, and Bedrich Hrozny still further east to the lands of the Hittites. And so it went up to our own times when the French businessman Maurice Giugnard claimed to have found the key in the Gothic, Guanche, and Old Norse languages by means of which he translated Etruscan into a curious French and an even more curious English. It is really not surprising that Professor Franz de Ruyt, Head of the Department of Etruscology at the University of Louvain, should, as it were, lose his academic temper and issue an angry statement to a professional journal condemning 'the ridiculous attempts of charlatans to decipher Etruscan that appear almost every year in many countries'.[1]

But despite the censure of the professors, amateurs continue to shut themselves in their studies and to examine the mysterious Etruscan script as the crypto-

A bilingual dedication in Latin and Punic over the main entrance to the great theatre of Leptis Magna in Tripoli.

Franz de Ruyt, 'L'état actuel des études étrusques', *Etudes Etrusco-Italiques* (Louvain: 1963), Series 4, Pt. 31, pp. 5 ff.

grapher examines a secret code. One recalls in this respect the young architect Michael Ventris, studying the strange symbols of Linear B and, significantly, being afraid to admit even to himself what he knew to be true – that Linear B was not Minoan but Greek. In fact, at one point Ventris thought that it was Etruscan, so he must have had a knowledge of this language and it is part of the tragedy of his premature and unnecessary death in an automobile accident that he did not live to tackle Etruscan with his brilliant cryptographic skills.

In the meantime, the more conventional philologists still hope that the indispensable bilingual will one day be found, though this, of course, depends on the success of archaeological investigations. If, for instance, the known sites of Etruscan cities had been methodically excavated during the nineteenth and early twentieth centuries, before they were lost under the conurbations of the later period, it is possible that a public monument in the two official languages, Etruscan and Latin, would have come to light. Such a tablet in Libyan and Latin is still in place over the main entrance to the theatre of Leptis Magna in Libya. But Etruscan archaeology, if it can be called that, has always consisted of tomb excavations which, significantly, have produced a number of bilinguals, though all of them limited to the names and ages of the interred. But the very fact that the later Etruscans did record their memorials in two languages indicates 175

that this was standard practice, certainly after the Roman conquest, as it was the practice in Libyan-speaking Africa and throughout the non-Greek-speaking provinces of that empire. Where, then, are the public plaques in two languages?

Such a memorial was indeed found recently at the old port of Pyrgi (today, Santa Marinella, an Italian seaside town) where excavations of an Etruscan temple dedicated to Uni produced a golden tablet inscribed in the Phoenician and Etruscan languages, the former of which is known. But evidently the two texts were not literal translations of each other, though the information they record is roughly identical. The temple dedication of Pyrgi does not take us much further in the quest for a key to the problem. Obviously something like the Rosetta Stone is needed: that is, a long bilingual text in Etruscan and Latin. Twenty years ago great hopes of finding such a memorial in the two languages were entertained by the French archaeologist Raymond Bloch, who was informed by a local farmer in Tuscany that he had found a column entirely covered with strange writing. The farmer stated that the letters of one section of the column were recognizable, but those of the other were completely unfamiliar to him. Bloch was understandably excited by this report, since the farmer owned land on an Etruscan site and, if his story were true, he had conceivably unearthed the long-sought-for bilingual. The French archaeologist with the farmer's help

A 5th-century Etruscan bronze helmet dedicated by Hieron of Syracuse to the temple at Olympia as war booty. The inscription is in Greek.

immediately began a thorough examination of all the stones which lay about on the surface of the designated field. When nothing resembling an inscribed block was found on the property, the excavator searched the surrounding fields, but still found nothing. M. Bloch appears to have become suspicious of his informant's facts and motives, and questioning him closely now learned that the Italian had done a bit of excavating himself, only without permission and therefore always at night. In short, he had prodded about in the tombs for treasure. But he could no longer remember the exact whereabouts of the mysterious column – either that, or it never existed. What did now exist, of course, was a Tuscan field neatly cleared of stones.

So without a Rosetta Stone to help them, or anything but the vaguest clues provided by the occasional bilingual, the Etruscologists were forced to conclude that the only possibility of understanding the language was to approach it as if it were a cypher. This approach, which has become known as the inductive or combinatory method, consists of comparing words of similar appearance with one another, trying to extract the root, and then tentatively guessing at the meaning. For instance, the words *ar, arθ, ara, araś, arce* are found in various texts or inscriptions, whence it is assumed that their root is *ar*, meaning 'to do'. Similarly *θezm, θezi, θezin, θezince, θereri* are said to have the root *θez* and to mean 'to make an offering'. *Tur, tura, ture, turi, turce*, are guessed at as forms of the verb 'to give'. This method has become almost a monopoly of the German

LEFT The Rosetta Stone, discovered in 1799, provided the clue to the decipherment of Old Egyptian. Etruscologists hope for a similar bilingual to enable them to understand Etruscan.

RIGHT A thin round plaque made of lead and inscribed with about seventy words; it reads from the outside edge towards the centre. No one has succeeded in translating this plaque.

and Italian philologists since 1879, when Wilhelm Deeke first stated the principle that 'Etruscan must be studied with the aid of Etruscan'. Strangely enough, the German savant changed his mind shortly after enunciating this principle and announced that the key to Etruscan would be found in Latin. But his first theory was the one that found most favour with the professional Etruscologists, who have become more and more scornful of attempts to relate Etruscan to any other language, they themselves preferring to go over and over the same Etruscan texts in the hope of breaking the cypher. They display amazing erudition and ingenuity in the process, but alas! do not illuminate with more than an occasional faint ray of light the still-impenetrable darkness which is the Etruscan language.

It is scarcely surprising that the search for a solution has led to so many alarms and excursions, great expectations and disappointments, accusations and even insults. As early as the eighteenth century we find Mario Guarnacci demanding that his rival Father Antonioli be deprived of a public office for daring to challenge his, Guarnacci's, theories. And in the nineteenth century the German Wolfgang Helbig insulted his Italian colleague Edoardo Brizio by stating that a scholarly journal was no place to refute the Italian's ridiculous theory of the Etruscans' origin. Signor Brizio replied in kind, and very soon the two scholars, the German and the Italian, were the leaders of two fierce factions locked in battle over the interpretation of some *minutia* of history. In fact, in another of these academic encounters, fought in the 1870s, Wilhelm Corssen's *Ueber die Sprache der Etrusker*, the fruit of many years of devoted study, was so mercilessly attacked by William Deeke that Corssen's untimely death at the age of fifty-three was said to have been caused by his colleague's derision. Ironically, Deeke himself eventually adopted Corssen's theory as to the Indo-Germanic nature of Etruscan, and in due course he received the same kind of treatment he had meted out to the author of *Ueber die Sprache*.

It will be obvious from all this academic to-ing and fro-ing that the problems implicit in the decipherment of Etruscan are probably the most difficult that the philologist faces today. And some idea of the complexity of the task can be gleaned from the seemingly simple problem of the identification of the Etruscan numbers one to six written on the six sides of a pair of dice found in 1848 in a tomb at Toscanella. It would appear at first sight that all one had to do was to find which was 'one' in order to identify the other five numbers. And since numbers are known in nearly every language of the world, the probability that a clue would be found here would seem high. But no such clue has ever been found, and in consequence controversy over the Toscanella dice has raged since the day of their discovery a hundred and twenty-five years ago.

The two dice, then, each have an identical Etruscan word written on each side of the six faces, whence the supposition that the words spell out the numbers one to six. The expression 'supposition' is used advisedly, since there are other

possibilities: the words may not refer to numbers at all – first, because it is not customary to spell out numbers on the face of a die, but to use indentations or pips; second, because the words could be the jargon used by dice players; and third, the Etruscan words may refer not to numbers but to objects, as in the dice game called Crown and Anchor in which the six faces are marked with an anchor, crown, club, diamond, heart, and spade.

But despite these objections, nearly all Etruscologists have automatically assumed that the words must refer to the numerals; and starting with this premise have tried to decide which word represents which number.

The six words written on the six faces of the two dice are:

$$ma\chi \text{ opposite } zal$$
$$\theta u \text{ opposite } hu\theta$$
$$ci \text{ opposite } \acute{s}a$$

Which of these words is 'one'?

It is a question we should be able to answer and could answer if only Etruscan could be related to some other specific language or family of languages. Thus, it is certain that the numbers one to ten, like words describing basic family relationships (father, mother, and so forth), are all derived from some common tongue both in the case of the Indo-European family of languages and in the case of the Semitic family. In addition, those philologists who maintain that *all* languages are derived originally from a common source examine the numerals of every language they can, whether living or dead, to get at least a hint of one of the Etruscan numbers. Searching through languages sometimes thousands of miles apart geographically, the savants who believe that *ma\chi* equals 'one' compare it with Armenian *mi*, Greek $\mu\acute{\iota}\alpha$, and even Mongolian *imak*. *Ci* which they say is 'three' is justified by reference to Circassian *tku*, Basque *hiru*, Berber *kerad*, and Egyptian χmt. On the other hand, those researchers who are convinced that Etruscan must belong to a particular family of languages produce

alternative evidence. The Reverend Isaac Taylor, Canon of York, who argued that Etruscan was an offshoot of what he calls North Turanian, 'proves' that *maχ* is one by comparing it with seventeen Tatar dialects: among them Tungusic where it is *amukon*, Motor where it is *om*, and Tymisch where it is *ockur*. By thumbing through the word lists of such curious tongues as Yenissei, Kamt-schadken, Thusci, Lapp, Zirianian, Tscherkess, Abase, Lesghi, Esth, Suomi, Samojedic, Wotiak, Tawgi, Anzuch, and a dozen or so more, Reverend Taylor arrives at his solution of the Toscanella dice mystery and collates the words with the numbers as follows:

$$maχ = \text{one}$$
$$ci \quad = \text{two}$$
$$zal = \text{three}$$
$$śa \quad = \text{four}$$
$$θu \quad = \text{five}$$
$$huθ = \text{six}$$

Notwithstanding this erudite clergyman's formidable array of languages, not a single philologist accepts his arguments, or, for that matter, the arguments of other colleagues. This is not surprising in view of the extraordinary theories put forward by even the most sober of scholars. For no less a savant than Professor Corssen, in his day the doyen of German philologists, seems to have had a mental aberration as a result of pondering the mystery of the Toscanella dice and to have read into the isolated words a complete Latin sentence as follows:

Magus	donarium	hoc	cisorio [facit]
Maχ	*θu-zal*	*huθ*	*ci-sa*

meaning 'Magus made this votive offering for Cisorius.'

The classical scholar Robert Ellis half accepted this solution, but preferred to read the words as Gaelic and made the donor of the gift not Magus but MacDougall. Canon Taylor, not to be outdone, finds the key to Corssen's sentence in Armenian and proposes 'Magus cuts the recompense of his vow.'

Finally, Alexander William Lindsay, twenty-fifth Earl of Crawford, arrived at a solution to this bogus anagram by taking some words from the Greek and some from the Gothic, to produce the curious though appropriate invocation 'May these sacred dice fall double sixes.'

But not surprisingly, the consensus was that all these interpretations were nonsense and that the dice were merely used for play and therefore had to be numbered. We know that dice throwing was as popular in the ancient world as it is today and that the arrangement of the pips was usually the same.

    one   two   three   four   five   six

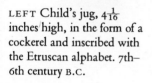

LEFT Child's jug, $4\frac{1}{16}$ inches high, in the form of a cockerel and inscribed with the Etruscan alphabet. 7th–6th century B.C.

RIGHT The base of a vase inscribed with Etruscan letters.

Moreover, the old writers declare that the marks must be placed so that the sum of the two numbers on opposite faces of the dice add up to seven. In other words, one is opposite to six; two to five; and three to four.

The probability is, then, that if we knew for certain the Etruscan word for 'one', we could find 'six' by looking at the opposite face. Similarly, if we knew the word for 'two', we could find 'five'; and the 'three' and 'four'. Unfortunately, the scholars cannot agree which number is 'one', although the majority have opted for *max*, since this is the only word which is written on each of the Toscanella dice in the same direction. If *max* is 'one', the *zal* on the opposite face is 'six'. If, again, the maker turned his die round by one face and marked the next square *θu*, this would give us 'two'. 'Five' must stand opposite 'two', so 'five' is *huθ*. Turning the die once again, the next face was presumably 'three', Etruscan *ci*. Opposite we find *śa* which is therefore 'four'. Imagine all six faces of a Toscanella die spread out flat so that they all could be seen at once, and the arrangement would look like this:

And the table arrived at by this method becomes:

max	=	one
θu	=	two
ci	=	three
śa	=	four
huθ	=	five
zal	=	six

Unfortunately, there is no way of proving this enumeration to be correct, and many leading Etruscologists do not accept it, but give their own value to

the series. And as if to make the problem more complicated, we get no help from the numerous funerary inscriptions which often give the age of the deceased. These inscriptions are comparatively easy to understand since, in common with tombstone epigraphs the world over, they usually consist of a formula along the lines of 'Here lies A, the son of B, died age so many years.' The Etruscans used a similar wording, giving the dead person's given name, the family name, the father's given name, and often the mother's given name. This list of names is sometimes followed by the word *ril* or *avil*, often used in conjunction with Roman numerals and, less frequently, with Etruscan numbers fully spelt out. Now in the former case, there is no difficulty in reading the inscription, as in this example:

> Partunus Vel Velθurus Satlnalc Ramθas
> clan avils lupu XXIIX[1]
> or: Vel Partunus, son of Velthur and Ramtha Satlana,
> died at the age of 28.

In other words, we know that *clan* in Etruscan means 'son'; *lupu*, 'died'; and

LEFT Bucchero vase with a chariot driver and horses.

RIGHT Votive dove in bronze with an Etruscan inscription. 3rd–2nd century B.C.

[1] *Corpus Inscriptionum Etruscarum* (1893–1936), 5424.

avils, 'years'. The Roman numeral XXIIX presents no problem. But the use of Roman numerals does not, of course, solve the mystery of the Etruscan numbers; and where we meet these, we are again in the dark, for the same reason that we are puzzled by the Toscanella dice. Thus, the funerary inscription of a certain Arnth Churcle actually gives this man's age at death in Etruscan numbers. It reads as follows:

Arnθ Xurcles Larθal clan . . . maχs semφalχls lupu[1]

or: Arnth Churchles, son of Larth . . . died aged ?

Again, we recognize the words *clan* and *lupu*, and we can assume that *maχs semφalχls* is the age at which Arnth died: i.e. a number. But what is it? Perhaps *maχs* is one, or a factor of one, but we have no clue whatsoever to *semφalχls*.

The end result is that since the experts cannot agree on even the words for the numerals one to six, there seems to be little chance of their agreeing on any aspect of the language. And this lack of general agreement has made all attempts at translating the key work of Etruscan literature, the Book of the Mummy, more or less doomed from the start, even though the theme of the work is certainly religious. In fact, the book appears to be some sort of church calendar, each chapter beginning with a date, and this assumption, based also on the frequent references to gods, is about all we have to go on at present; and the professional Etruscologists now admit that they cannot do more than make an educated guess at the actual contents of the book. Certainly the method of trying to read Etruscan by comparing it with itself, a method which has been worked at for a hundred years, can offer no further useful results. One reaches the point of staring at words like *al*, *ale*, *alce*, *alice*, *aliqu*, *alpan*, *alpnu*, assuming that the root is *al*, and then trying to find the meaning of one form from another similar form. Obviously the *meaning* of the root word will not reveal itself by this method, however long one stares at the apparent variations. One practitioner of this combinatory method takes the word *raθχ*, for instance, and translates it 'to the left(?)'. The question mark he inserts automatically suggests that *raθχ* could equally well mean 'to the right(?)', or 'forward(?)' or 'backwards(?)', until one can only conclude that such guesses are a waste of time.

The plain fact is that an unknown language can only be deciphered by comparing it with a known language. The decipherment of Egyptian, Babylonian, and Linear B proves the point.[2] And for this reason, the non-professionals, who are not bound by the narrow rules which seem to govern academic Etruscologists, continue to look for the key in all sorts of other tongues, even though the most erudite of them has never convinced a single person other than his disciples that he has succeeded. The professionals, as we have seen, make short work of these attempts at translating the Book of the Mummy, attempts which appear periodically as the brain children of all manner of enthusiastic laymen – philosophers, priests, even businessmen – who have become obsessed

[1] *Corpus Inscriptionum Italicarum* (1867). 2070.

[2] The mystery of Linear B was finally solved by Michael Ventris when he proved that the *language*, though written in an unknown script, was Greek. Once this was established, despite the opposition of orthodox classicists, translation was straightforward.

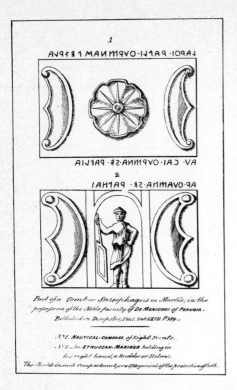

Part of a Tomb or Sarcophagus in Marble, in the
possession of the Noble family of De Meniconi of Perugia.
Published in Dempster, tom 1. tab LXVII P.389.

No 1. NAUTICAL COMPASS of Eight Points.
No 2. An ETRUSCAN MARINER holding in
his right hand, a Rudder or Helm.
The Shields in each Compartment, are Allegorical of the protection of both.

Translation

In the night on a voyage out or home in sailing happen
always in clear weather is known the course of going

A BRONZE ETRUSCO-PHŒNICIAN

NAUTICAL COMPASS.

In the Museum at Florence.

The above is half the size of the Original.

Illustrations from Sir William Betham's book *Etruria-Celtica* 'proving' that the Etruscans used the compass to navigate their ships to Ireland.

by the mystery of the Etruscan language as others have become obsessed by the whereabouts of Atlantis, the Garden of Eden, or the Holy Grail. One is bound to admit that, reading these translations, the critics have a point: for the most part they are almost as incomprehensible as the original.

One reason may be that the would-be translators seem to have looked for a key in the dictionaries of obscure languages whose vocabulary and phonology are not wholly understood themselves; favourite languages being Egyptian, Old Albanian, Old Scandinavian, archaic Finnish, primitive Basque, or the Guanche of the Canary Islands. The process of thumbing through the dictionaries and torturing the chosen word into strange forms to make it resemble the hoped-for meaning usually results in what can only be described as gibberish. Here are four translations of the famous incantation at the beginning of the seventh chapter of the Zagreb manuscript.

The original Etruscan reads:

> ceia hia
> > etnam ciz vacl trin vale
> male ceia hia
> > etnam ciz vacle aisvale
> male ceia hia
> > trin etnam ciz ale
> male ceia hia
> > etnam ciz vacle vile vale

The first translation was made in 1913 by Jules Martha, a Professor of Literature at the University of Paris, ten years or so after the publication of the text of the Zagreb mummy by the German scholars who first identified it as being written in Etruscan.[1] M. Martha chose Finnish as his key and arrived at this:

Crie! de l'énergie!
Tantôt l'apostrophe: Bien éclatant, élève la voix! Attention!
Crie! de l'énergie!
Tantôt l'apostrophe: augmente convenablement (la voix)! Attention!
Crie! de l'énergie! de la sonorité!
Tantôt l'apostrophe: trop bas! Attention![1]

A rendering into English of this near-incomprehensible French might be as follows:

Shout! Energetically!
Now make the response: very loudly, raise your voice! Take heed!
Shout! Energetically!
Now make the response: shout as loud as you can! Take heed!
Shout! Energetically! Sonorously!
Now make the response: too low! Take heed!

A decade or so later, a Capuchin friar called Hilaire de Barenton put forward the theory that the Book of the Mummy was a version of the Egyptian Book of the Dead and that the Etruscan language was a dialect of ancient Egypt. Hilaire was an Egyptologist (albeit an unorthodox one since he maintained that the Chinese lived in Egypt, though they were driven out very early in history, to be followed by the English, the Basques, the Latins, and finally the Greeks and Russians). On the strength of his acquaintance with hieroglyphics, he set to work to identify all the Etruscan words of the Mummy text with Egyptian roots and in this manner laboriously translated the Zagreb manuscript into French. It follows that the Friar's translation based on Old Egyptian is bound to be very different from Professor Martha's rendering based on Old Finnish, as a comparison of the two versions made from the famous incantation passage will show:

Le feu a jeté ses rayons,
Viens distribuer la nourriture.
Projette la lumière
Sur le germe de ton sein.
O visage de vautour,
Aux yeux de vautour,
Accorde qu'il monte.
Le feu a jeté ses rayons,
Viens distribuer la nourriture.
Projette la lumière sur le germe de ton sein;
C'est le germe du grand générateur. Qu'il parte et monte,
Accorde qu'il monte.
Le feu a jeté ses rayons,
Vautour en ton visage,
Viens distribuer la nourriture[2]

[1] Jules Martha, *La Langue Étrusque* (Paris: E. Leroux, 1913), pp. 308 ff.
[2] Hilaire de Barenton, *La Texte Étrusque de la Momie d'Agram*, Études Orientales No. 6 (Paris: Maisonneuve, 1929), pp. 48–51.

Which we put into English as:

The fire has thrown out its gleams,
Proceed with the distribution of the food.
Project the light
Upon the seed of thy womb.
O face of the vulture,
With the eyes of a vulture,
Let him rise up.
The fire has thrown out its gleams,
Proceed with the distribution of food.
Project the light on the seed of thy womb;
It is the seed of the great generator. May he come forth and rise up,
Let him rise up.
The fire has thrown out its gleams, . . .

All these references to fire, food, vulture, and the like are explained by the Friar as part of the Etruscan ritual of the vulture goddess. Hence he translates the Etruscan word *trin* as *visage de vautour* on the grounds that it consists of two Coptic words, *tre* (meaning 'vulture') and *an* (meaning 'face'). And since many readers might have been puzzled by the appearance on the scene of a vulture, Hilaire explains that 'O, face of the vulture' refers to the bird's skin with which the vulture goddess was covered in the Etruscan 'Rite of the Holocaust', a rite, according to the translator, which derived from the worship of the Egyptian gods Mut and Amon. The Capuchin's mythology tends to get quite complicated, but his etymology is relatively simple, for he takes a single word like *etnam* which occurs frequently in the Book of the Mummy and makes of it an entire sentence: *Viens distribuer la nourriture*. So the one word *aisvale* becomes *c'est le germe du grand générateur: qu'il parte et monte*.

The reaction of Hilaire's colleagues to his translation of the Etruscan manuscript is not on record; but it is likely that they kept quiet out of respect for the cloth, which they did not feel required to do in the case of Maurice Guignard, who published his Etruscan researches in 1963 under the title of *Comment J'ai Déchiffré la Langue Étrusque*. Guignard, a French businessman who dabbled in arcane subjects like the Lydian language (*How I Deciphered the Lydian Language*), Messapian (*How I Deciphered the Messapian Language*), and the Norse colonization of Normandy, seems to have been unable to make up his mind whether Etruscan was related to Old Scandinavian, Old Finnish, Basque, or the Guanche of the Canaries. And since he argues that 'the Albanians are the descendants of the ancient Etruscans', presumably Old Albanian should be added to his list of relevant languages. Guignard has provided us in *Comment J'ai Déchiffré* with English versions of his French translations from the Etruscan. For instance, his English translation of the famous inscription on the mirror which portrays the adult Hercules being suckled by Juno is: 'Hercules, a

Gold votive tablet, one of three, found during recent excavations of the 5th century B.C. Etruscan Temple of Uni (the Roman Juno). The temple was unearthed at Pyrgi, the port of inland cities like Cerveteri, Veii, and Tarquinia. The language of two of the tablets is Etruscan. The third plaque is in Punic.

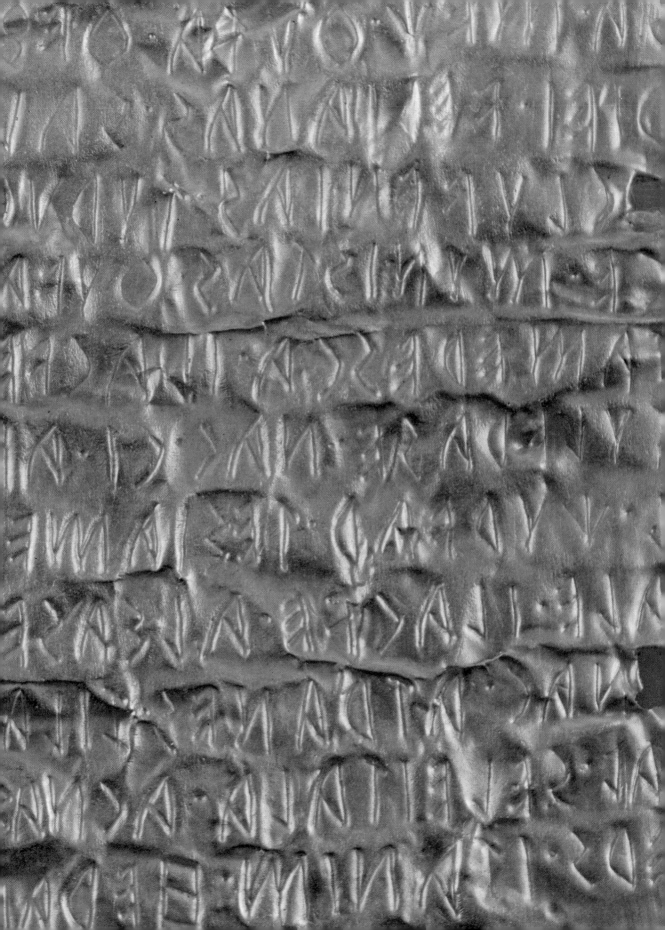

Pediment from the Temple of Uni at Pyrgi, showing the battle between the gods – Zeus and Athena – and the giants.

joyful man, calling himself vigorous, is tapping gluttedly the woman sitting on the stool.'

Here, then, is Guignard's English rendering of the *male ceia hia* incantation from the Book of the Mummy:

> Stride with frenzy, bewitch the banquet, three times upset,
> In cadence stride with frenzy, bewitch the banquet, furiously wail.
> In cadence stride three times then with frenzy, bewitch the temple.
> In cadence stride three times with frenzy, bewitch the banquet, wildly wail.
> Sing, turn into troll with frenzy, bewitch then three times this missing.[1]

Maurice Guignard, however, has not said the last word. In fact, his theory that Etruscan is related to a language he calls Urnordic whose descendant is Icelandic is rejected by Dr Zacharie Mayani of the University of Paris who has revived the once-popular Albanian as the key which can unlock the Etruscan mystery. His rendering of the *male ceia hia* passage is as follows:

> Call the shades!
> Call to the shades of the fathers: Live again!
> A feast for noble heroes!
> Loudly call the shades of the fathers: Live again!
> This is a feast of the divine [shades].
> Loudly call the shades of the heroic fathers.
> Let them live again [?].
> Loudly call the shades of the fathers: Live again!
> A feast! revolve and dance! Halt! Change the pattern!
> O shades of heroes, live again.[2]

After reading these four translations of the same passage we can understand better the indignation as well as the frustration of those Etruscologists who stick tenaciously to the old combinatory method, particularly as their most authoritative exponent, Alfredo Trombetti, was unable to make head or tail of these *male ceia hia* verses, except to suggest that the rhyming word-pairs *ale-male*; *vile-vale* aroused echoes of Basque *aiko-maiko*; Georgian *are-mare*; and Turkish *et-met*. But Trombetti made no attempt to translate the famous incantation, thus admitting by implication that the orthodox method simply did not work, which may account for the harsh words his followers have to say about the efforts of outsiders like Dr Mayani, whose translation was described as *una incredibile stupidaggine* ('an unbelievable piece of foolishness') by one critic. But obviously something has gone wrong with all four of the translations cited above; or, at least, all four cannot be right if the same line *ceia hia* comes out as:

> Shout! Energetically! (Martha)
> The fire has thrown out its gleams (Hilaire)
> Stride with frenzy (Guignard)
> Call the shades of the fathers (Mayani)

[1] Maurice Guignard, *Comment J'ai Déchiffré la Langue Étrusque* (Pultelange-lès-Thionville: published by the author, 1962), pp. 36–7.
[2] Zacharie Mayani, *The Etruscans Begin to Speak*, trans. Patrick Evans (London: Souvenir Press, 1962), pp. 312 ff.

191

In each case, of course, the dictionary employed by the translator has deter-mined the outcome, together with a little bit of tinkering with the required meaning. Martha therefore sees the Finnish word *kaje* as equating with Etruscan *ceia*; Hilaire goes to the Egyptian *kaHa*; Guignard to the 'Urnordic' *skaeva*; and Mayani to the Albanian *kjaj*. The consensus can only be that these searchers for the Etruscans have made a people whom we have tried so long and so hopefully to understand seem even more remote and unreal.

And so it is arguable that many seekers after the Etruscans have ended their journey by losing themselves and us in the *terra incognita* of the Etruscan language. Clearly the majority of them have fallen into that philological trap of 'proving', by hook or by crook, what they have already assumed. Sir William Betham, the nineteenth-century Irish antiquarian, is perhaps the classic victim of this pitfall for, not content with insisting that Etruscan was a close relation of Celtic, he 'proved' that the Etruscan mariners steered their ships to Ireland by means of the magnetic compass. Betham's 'compass' was an eight-branched candelabra which was exhibited in the museum at Florence and which the Irishman had seen only in illustration. And even though the learned world of the 1840s was not as dogmatic in the field of Etruscology as it is today and was prepared to listen to any new theory by scholars, whether professional or amateur, critics lost all patience with Sir William when he insisted that the Latin of a bilingual inscription found in the Tomb of the Volumnii at Perugia was a forgery. His reason? The Latin text did not give the same meaning as his translation of the Etruscan from Old Irish.

Even so, there is nothing to prevent those with a special aptitude for crypto-graphy from tackling Etruscan, which is the last of the important languages to require translating. It must, after all, belong to *some* linguistic family, for whether the people who spoke it came from Asia Minor or were native to Italy, they were certainly related to one or the other sub-group of the three main races of mankind. And if one day some philological genius does solve the mystery, we shall at last be able to enter more intimately into the inner life of the Etruscans themselves, even if their surviving literature consists mainly of official pronounce-ments, largely religious in content. The Etruscans, after all, were a theocentric people whose lives were regulated by ritual, so until we know what that ritual was, we cannot expect fully to understand either their political or social institutions.

In the meantime, for those who are attracted by the realities as well as the mysteries of this unusual nation, there remains the opportunity for a pilgrimage to Etruria itself. We shall therefore end our Etruscan journey by visiting those places which still speak to us in a more human and intelligible language than either their writings or their exhibits in the museum showcases.

Bolsena today, site of the Etruscan Volsinii, where the slaves revolted in the 3rd century B.C.

Part Three
The Modern Traveller's Guide
to Etruscan Places

CHAPTER ELEVEN

Touring the Hill Towns of Etruria

A PILGRIMAGE to the ancient seats of this nation is certainly easy enough to undertake today in comparison with the difficulties experienced by the early travellers. On the other hand, one must admit that the rewards are correspondingly fewer.

First, as we have seen, the plundering during the nineteenth century of nearly all the most beautiful or archaeologically significant sites has greatly diminished the 'presence' of the Etruscans – that presence which we can still sense throughout the Greek and Roman world, thanks to the survival of their temples, theatres, and other public monuments. Second, the onrush of modern progress has finished what the pickaxes of the first excavators began, and no-where is the effect of these two processes more apparent than at Tarquinia. We know that when the necropolis at Tarquinia was first opened up at the end of the eighteenth century, the excavators destroyed scores of painted tombs whose locations, like their contents, have now completely disappeared. Two centuries later this once small and secluded hill town, which should have been preserved as the Athens of Etruria, has become a stopover for sightseers whose motor coaches – and litter – make a visit to Tarquinia more of an ordeal than a pilgrimage.

Yet it is still possible for those travellers who are prepared to forego the standard sights to enter into a closer communion with the Etruscans. For this, they should choose a less publicized centre for their headquarters, from which they can make excursions into a landscape which has so far escaped the blight of commercialism. The Tuscan town of Arezzo on the borders of Umbria is such an agreeable centre, for it is within easy distance of Cortona, Montepulciano, Chiusi, and Florence, all of which places the Etruscan explorer will no doubt wish to visit. It is true that Arezzo itself belongs more to the Middle Ages than to the Etruscan founders; and even though it was one of the Twelve Cities, nothing remains of the original Arretium except sections of the famous brick wall which surrounded the city – famous since it is the only example of the use of brick by the Etruscans who invariably built with the local stone. The museum houses what else is left of the ancient site, which was one of the richest of Etruria, yielding enough treasure to enrich public and private collections throughout Tuscany. The most valuable and famous of the finds, the bronze Chimaera and the Minerva, dis-

The famous 'Chimera', now in the Archaeological Museum, Florence, was discovered in 1534 near Arezzo, which is still a pleasant centre for the Etruscan traveller.

covered in or near Arezzo in 1534, are now in the Museo Archeologico of Florence. Nor is it clear where most of the other artefacts in the Arezzo Museum came from since there are no tombs in the immediate vicinity of the city itself, though the surrounding hills, for those who are willing to walk over them, are strewn with fragments of pottery and ancient walls belonging to a whole complex of towns, villages, and farms which made up the Etruscan city-state.

Twenty-five miles south of Arezzo stands Cortona, in legend the most ancient city in Italy, supposedly built before Troy, and undoubtedly once the mightiest city of all Etruria. Here the traveller can begin to feel the actual presence of the Etruscans, whose enormous walls encircle the town for a circumference of two miles. The best place to see these Cyclopean defences is at the highest point of the city, just below the medieval fortress whose foundations belong to the Etruscan period. And if one arrives in Cortona on a Sunday morning in spring during the service in the eleventh-century cathedral, one can wander through the ancient town which George Dennis found so cheerless and melancholy and look out over one of the most magnificent views in central Italy – a vast tract of countryside, once even more highly cultivated and spotted with farms than it is today. The terrace in front of the Church of St Margherita used to be a favourite resting place of those nineteenth-century travellers who climbed the steep hill to Cortona. Here they dutifully enjoyed and described in their 195 letters home a panoramic view of the Umbrian mountains and the hill towns of Tuscany and, to the south, the glittering Lake of Trasimene on whose shores Hannibal annihilated the Roman army.

Cortona, as well as being the oldest city of Italy, has the oldest antiquarian society, the Accademia Etrusca, founded in the mid-eighteenth century and active ever since. The museum of the Academy is one of the most attractive in Italy, partly because of the Renaissance palace in which it is housed, partly because of the surprising treasures it contains, and partly because the visitor has the place almost all to himself. The relics belong to an archaic period, which is probably why they stayed in Cortona and were not sold to foreign collectors. The elongated bronze figurines, which remind us of the *nuraghi* bronzes of Sardinia on the one hand and the sculptures and paintings of some modern artists on the other, were regarded as of little aesthetic value by the antique dealers of the nineteenth century, though today, following the wide swings of fashion and taste, they would be considered the most interesting of the Etruscan sculptures. But neither fashion nor changes in taste can add to or detract from the wonder of the great bronze candelabrum of the Cortona Museum, perhaps the most remarkable of all Etruscan manufactures. This candelabrum is a round bowl two feet in diameter with sixteen lamps suspended from the rim, the lamps being fed by oil from the main bowl. At the bottom of each lamp is alternately the figure of a winged siren in relief and a satyr playing the double pipes. Between each lamp is cast the head of the horned and bearded Dionysus. Elsewhere the candelabrum is decorated with lions, leopards, wolves, and griffins in pairs devouring a bull, a horse, a boar, and a stag, while another band on the rim shows dolphins sporting in the sea. Between two of the lamps is a short inscription in Etruscan apparently reading *tinscvil*, the word which is written on the Arezzo Chimaera. We recognize in the first syllable, *Tin*, the name of the Etruscan god corresponding to the Greek Zeus and the Roman Jupiter. The last part of the word, *vil*, reminds us of the constantly repeated phrase *vile vale* found in the liturgical Book of the Mummy, so we can guess at some such meaning as 'Hail to Tin', suggesting that the candelabrum hung in an Etruscan temple which also housed the Chimaera. Both objects were probably carried off when the temple was destroyed, perhaps during the civil war between Caesar and Pompey, perhaps during the invasion of Totila the Vandal. Gibbon suggests a third cause for the destruction of the pagan temples and the scattering of their treasures – the abhorrence of the Catholic Church during the ninth and tenth centuries for the old gods and their shrines; or, as he puts it, 'the statues, altars, and houses of the daemons were an abomination in their eyes.' Whatever the reasons for the destruction of the temple of the Etruscan Jupiter, all that survived was the Chimaera and the candelabrum discovered by accident in a ditch not far from Cortona in 1840, three hundred years after the Chimaera came to light some-where in the vicinity. The candelabrum was bought for a large sum (seven

ABOVE The Arco
d'Augusto, Perugia,
showing a succession of
architectural styles from
the Etruscan to the
Renaissance period.

OPPOSITE Votive figure
in bronze of a girl
holding a serpent. This
elongated style was
popular from the 4th to
the 2nd century B.C. A
masterpiece of Etruscan
bronze work.

OVERLEAF A drawing
made by George Dennis
of the famous Cortona
candelabrum. The heads
of the horned and
bearded Bacchus are
shown.

hundred dollars, worth at least ten times that amount today) by a Signora
Tommasi of Cortona who presented it to the Accademia Etrusca on her death.
It is fortunate that this unique relic was unearthed at this particular period,
since by the 1840s the peasants who were continually finding Etruscan artefacts
knew the value of the various objects being taken from the ground and so
instead of throwing the mass of corroded bronze away as an impediment to
their ploughs, saved from certain destruction the most beautiful and wonderful
of Etruscan bronzes.

From Cortona the traveller passes through some of the most beautiful scenery
in Italy, through a landscape which enshrines one of the most dramatic events in
the history of the ancient world: the defeat of the Roman army by the Carthaginian
invaders. The interested student can, with the aid of Livy, Polybius, and other
historians of Republican Rome, reconstruct for himself the events of the great
battle in which the Consul Flaminius led his legions into a trap and was
surrounded by Hannibal's Numidian cavalry and Balearic slingers. Fifteen
thousand Roman soldiers died on the plain of Trasimene; six thousand were
captured; and ten thousand fled back to Rome.

The Etruscans, of course, were not involved in this battle, since by the second
century B.C. they had ceased to exist as an independent nation. But we can
imagine that they watched the battle from their cities and settlements overlooking 197

the lake with mixed emotions, for they had once been allies of the Carthaginians against the Romans, though now forcibly conjoined with the latter people in a united Italy. No doubt a number of the Roman legionaries who fled from the battlefield after their commander Flaminius was killed sought refuge inside the great walls of Cortona, Chiusi, and Perugia, three cities which had belonged to the Confederation of the Twelve. Those who escaped to Perugia passed through the same city gates that the traveller passes through today, though every conqueror since the Etruscans has added to these defensive portals, which now represent the work of Roman, medieval, and Renaissance military architects. The twentieth-century contribution is a tangle of overhead wires and an assortment of traffic signs plastered all over the façade of the most ancient of the gates, the celebrated Arco d'Augusto.

Perugia was one of the twelve Etruscan cities which never lost its importance as a provincial capital of central Italy, and it seems always to have been a large and wealthy centre of succeeding ages. It reached the heights of its architectural glory during the Renaissance which has left its memorials in the form of the magnificent cathedral, a hundred churches, and the works of Perugino and the Umbrian school. At the same time, it was inevitable that the growth of Perugia from Roman times onwards has gradually effaced nearly all traces of the Etruscan citizens whose distinguished families, buried in the surrounding rock tombs, are still at least known to us by name and even by appearance. The Etruscans of Perugia cremated their dead and deposited the ashes in funerary urns on the lids of which was sculpted an effigy of the deceased. The tourist can experience a momentary communion with this lost people in the Hypogeum of the Volumnii family at the bottom of the hill on which Perugia stands – that is, once he is inside the tomb and out of sight of the concrete autostrada which is now being

built over the top of it. This celebrated burial vault has an inscription cut into one of the stone doors which transcribed into Roman characters reads:

ARNTH LARTH VELIMNAS ARUNEAL PHUSIUR

SUTAI ACIL PRECE [or, THECE]

whose general meaning can be guessed at as 'Arnth and Larth of the family Volumnii built and dedicated this tomb.' Here were buried members of this powerful clan: fathers, mothers, and children, together with some of their personal possessions. Their ashes were placed in cinerary urns on the lid of which each of the deceased is shown reclining on a couch, a chaplet round his brow, a torque round his neck, and a wine goblet in his hand. So the noble Etruscans wished to be remembered.

The other relics of Etruscan Perugia are housed in the Civic Museum; and for those who wish to wrestle once again with the mysterious language, there is a *cippus*, or stone marker comprising forty-six lines of a hundred and thirty words carefully carved and coloured red. Nobody apart from Sir William Betham has managed to translate this document: but the Irishman, applying his Celtic theory, announced it was a 'Notice to Mariners about to Undertake the Voyage across the Bay of Biscay to Carne in Ireland'. Since Perugia is two hundred miles from the west Italian coast and some two thousand miles by sea from Ireland, it seems strange that these navigational instructions should have been set up in an inland city. More cautious scholars prefer the theory that it concerns agricultural boundaries in the region.

Many of the other tombs which were found during the nineteenth century in the Perugian hillsides, nearly all of them containing urns, funerary furniture, and ornaments, have been lost or abandoned, for it was reported at the time that the

ABOVE A chariot race. Detail from a wall painting at Chiusi.

OPPOSITE The mausoleum of the hero Lars Porsena at Chiusi. A drawing based on the description of Varro.

local antiquaries accumulated such a vast collection of Etruscan artefacts that they were unable to dispose of them at good market prices. It is unlikely now that the archaeologists will have either the time or resources to methodically explore this rich necropolis.

From Perugia the traveller goes westward to the next of the principal cities of the Etruscan Confederation – to Chiusi, the Clusium of the Romans and Camars of the Etruscans. Chiusi was the capital of Lars Porsena whose very name, we are told by the Roman historians themselves, struck terror into the Senate and Roman people. But that was two thousand five hundred years ago, and today Chiusi is a quiet little country town which retains its Etruscan city gate and the massive walls which still encircle the city. The tunnels or conduits which issue from these walls seem to be part of a subterranean system of reservoirs and sewers which are still hidden under the old foundations. Indeed, it is rumoured that the Tomb of Lars Porsena is underneath the cathedral, for some such tomb is described by the encyclopedist Varro, who may even have seen the ruins of the monument. At any rate, according to Varro the base of Porsena's sepulchre was three hundred feet square and fifty feet high, inside which was built a labyrinth, no doubt intended to outwit the tomb robbers. On top of this base stood five pyramids, one at each corner and one in the centre of the square, all of them a hundred and fifty feet high. And this was not all. The points of the four pyramids at the corners of the base were joined by a bronze girder and on the

201

circle thus formed four more pyramids, each a hundred feet high, were erected. Over this second storey of pyramids was built a floor supporting still another five pyramids 'the height of which Varro was ashamed to mention,' says Pliny, which well he might have been, since the structure had become manifestly fabulous. One can understand why the majority of commentators have dismissed the description as nonsense, even if a learned priest called Angelo Cortenovis wrote a treatise proving that such an erection must have been a giant electric generator.

But for somebody who has the interest as well as the time to search for the evidence of such marvels, Chiusi and the surrounding country offer a whole subterranean world for exploration, because this region is one of the richest of the Etruscan sites, with new tombs having been discovered within the last decades and others undoubtedly still to be found. The most remarkable of the known tombs, the excavation of which led in 1839 to a renewed interest in the Mausoleum of Porsena, is the tomb known as the Poggio Gaiella, a curious necropolis inside a conical hill three miles to the north-east of Chiusi. On burrowing into the hillside, the original excavators were naturally struck by the labyrinthine nature of this burial place, which coincided in some respects with Varro's description of Porsena's tomb. But apart from the statement that the Etruscan King's monument was built on 'an inextricable labyrinth', the Poggio Gaiella cemetery has nothing resembling the elaborate pyramidal construction of the legendary mausoleum. It does, however, have an underground network of at least forty sepulchral chambers arranged in three levels and interconnected by a bewildering system of tunnels. These tunnels – some of which complete a circle from the main burial chamber, while others connect one tomb with another, and still others end without going anywhere at all – are nearly all of regular though small dimensions, roughly three feet high and two feet wide and therefore just large enough to permit a small man to creep through on all fours. What, then, was the object of these subterranean passages? The answer that comes at once to mind is that they were driven through the rock by tomb robbers at some unknown date. On the other hand, many of them are so carefully and even curiously made that one is entitled to ask whether the robbers would have spent so much skill and time in tunnelling in this fashion; for in one case a passage diminishes progressively as it advances – not at random, but by regular stages, as though each section had been made to fit into its predecessor, as the tubes of a collapsible telescope fit into each other.

The necropolis of Poggio Gaiella had certainly been rifled before it was opened in 1839, for the confusion inside was obviously the result of thieves rummaging hurriedly through the treasures which had been deposited alongside the coffins and urns of the dead. As usual, these thieves had carried off only articles made in precious metals, throwing such objects as urns, vases, and pots of one sort and another on the ground. However, they left a rich harvest for the

Porta all'Arco, the Etruscan gate at Volterra, with three unidentifiable heads affixed to the arch. 2nd century B.C.

nineteenth-century excavators, especially of vases, including the magnificent one depicting the Judgment of Paris, found in a hundred and twenty pieces and skilfully restored by Italian artisans. They found, too, various items of gold and jewellery which the tomb robbers had overlooked and, most interesting of all, an assortment of the curious *canopi*, cinerary urns in the form of a crude sculpture of the deceased whose head formed the lid of the container while his arms, reduced in size, formed the handles. So the number of tombs in this mysterious necropolis and the amount of treasure that was buried in them suggests that either some prince or noble family of the city was buried here when Chiusi was the most powerful member of the Etruscan league – from the fifth to the third century B.C.

There are a great many other unusual tombs in the vicinity of Chiusi and, indeed, rock chambers are still being discovered, the latest of them, the Tomb of the Pellegrina, having been left by the excavators as it was found, with the sarcophagi still on the stone benches in the various chambers and niches. So here the traveller feels, in such peaceful and unspoilt surroundings, something of the presence of the Etruscans, not only in their graves, but in the fields and groves of this pleasant countryside. Indeed, the whole region is rich in beauty as well as history, with almost every hill crowned by those little walled towns which, judging from the surrounding cemeteries, were flourishing Etruscan settlements two thousand five hundred years ago. Cetona, Sarteano, Chianciano, and Monte-pulciano are all built on lofty heights amid wheatfields, olive groves, and vine-yards such as the Etruscans themselves must have cultivated; and from the languid expression of the revellers at their banquets in so many of the tomb paintings, with couples holding cups to each others' lips, they knew the delights of the local vintage. Nor presumably would they have found the religious legends of this region as odd as we moderns do on learning that the Church of San Bigio outside the walls of Montepulciano was erected to commemorate the miracle of the Madonna whose soulful eyes caused the very cattle in the fields to kneel reverently before her image.

From Montepulciano one can go by the old Via Flaminia, named after the consul who died at Lake Trasimene along with the flower of the Roman army, to Viterbo by way of Orvieto, that gem of the Middle Ages with the most elegant of all Italian cathedrals, glorified with the frescos of Fra Angelico and Luca Signorelli. So much architectural beauty, so many magnificent churches, palaces, piazzas, and treasures of medieval and Renaissance art do not speak to us of those silent Etruscans we are seeking; but they were undoubtedly here, for their tombs riddle the great rock of red tufo on which Orvieto is built. Yet even the name of this Etruscan settlement is unknown, and the city, in any case, has no visible evidence of the Etruscan presence.

One therefore presses on to Viterbo with its memories of the Dominican friar Giovanni Nanni, who was among the first of the old antiquarians to draw the world's attention to the lost Etruscan race, impostor though he is said to have

Stone cinerary urn of the late 6th century. The final phase of the canopic-jar style is represented here. A head of the deceased forms the lid of the container and the arms form handles.

been. Viterbo is the headquarters for a visit to Castel d'Asso where we are again in the open air and above ground among the people we are searching for. Castel d'Asso is a wide valley overhung by a ruined castle, and all along its cliffs the Etruscans cut the façades of their tombs in the form of houses which, unlike the temple tombs of Norchia, are Egyptian in character. The false doors to these house tombs are wider at the bottom than at the top, and they have inscribed over them the names of the families whose sepulchres they were. The actual grave chambers are reached by a flight of steps cut into the rock underneath the façade; and they were apparently left open, perhaps for the funeral feast or for the visits of relatives to the grave. At the back of the entrance chamber is another false door, again cut into the rock Egyptian style and often panelled; underneath this door is a tunnel which leads down into the tomb itself. As the tomb is usually a simple hole inside the cliff it is obvious that Castel d'Asso is one of the most archaic of the Etruscan cemeteries. It is also one of the most beautiful and one of the loneliest, and for this reason repays the traveller who does not mind walking through a deserted countryside.

We have already discussed the near-by necropolis of Norchia, visited from Vetralla, just thirteen miles southwards from Viterbo. Norchia, with its great temple tombs, resembles Castel d'Asso scenically, for it too is a valley the cliff-sides of which were utilized by the Etruscan architects. A comparable necropolis which has a fascinating variety of cliff tombs can be visited at Blera. Some are sculpted in the form of temples, some as houses, and some as columbaria, with niches in which the cinerary urns were placed as in Roman times. As is usual with all these unspoilt corners of rural Italy, Blera still has its ruined castle dominating the valleys and glens; these castles were the palaces of various counts and feudal lords of the region. Even when George Dennis visited Blera in 1845, the Duke of Bieda and Count of St Giorgio had absolute power over his tenants, even over their lives and properties. But he did not abuse his position as, evidently, his ancestor had done three centuries before, for this nobleman, insist-ing on his *ius primae noctis* (or, as Dennis puts it, 'forestalling every bridegroom in their domain') had his palace, whose ruins we see today, burnt down by the peasants.

It is not far from the tranquil valleys of Castel d'Asso, Norchia, and Blera to Tarquinia, the most famous and popular of the Etruscan sites, once called the Queen of the Maremma. As we have said elsewhere, it is a town to avoid at weekends and during the height of the tourist season, though it must be visited by all who are intrigued by things Etruscan, if only to see the terracotta winged horses in the municipal museum. On a quiet day in early spring, however, Tarquinia reveals to the traveller familiar with the early history of Etruscan exploration something of the excitement it had for those antiquaries and artists who came here soon after the wonderful painted tombs were discovered towards the end of the eighteenth century. For there is nothing in all the ruins of the

Bronze votive figurines of helmeted warriors from the 5th century B.C. These stylized statuettes, cast solid, were produced in great numbers by Etruscan bronze-workers from the 7th to the 3rd century B.C.

classical world which excels the frescos of such subterranean art galleries as the Tomb of the Leopards, the Lionesses, the Bulls, the Augurs, the Shields, the Inscriptions, and many others which the visitor is taken to see if the official guide can be bothered to conduct him on the complete rounds. And one uses the term 'art galleries' advisedly, since the walls of the Tarquinian burial chambers were decorated with scenes from almost every aspect of Etruscan life as if for an exhibition of topical paintings. The impression one gets from these pictures is of the vitality and sheer gaiety of the ancient people who drew them, and it is for this reason that a visit to the Tarquinian necropolis is essential, if only to balance the effect created by those sometimes wearisome tours of the museums. Here in the tombs the shades at least of the Etruscans live again: the girl at the banquet table throws her arms passionately round the neck of her lover, the dancers whirl about, the flute player blows his double pipes, boys dive into the sea, a well-fed cat crouches under the table. All these scenes of merriment are intermingled with the symbolism of death, so that here the whole system of the Etruscan life view would be illustrated for us if we were able to interpret it. But it is certain that we have come so far in two thousand five hundred years away from this mystical concept of man's fate that any interpretation can only be guesswork, for how can we explain an attitude towards death which combines at one and the same time so much gaiety with so many horrors?

From Tarquinia one goes north to Monte Argentario via Vulci, that desolate necropolis which enriched the speculators of the last century and has now been left to the local farmers and an occasional tourist. True, Italian archaeologists are to re-excavate some of these old sites, and digs have been, or are being made at Vulci, Veii, Rusellae, the cities of the Po Valley, and of both the Adriatic and Tyrrhenian coasts. But trained archaeologists are in short supply in Italy as everywhere else and, while funds are forthcoming from the government, the numbers of voluntary helpers on whom the directors of archaeological projects depend is inadequate. Is it the case that Italians, having so many ruins throughout the length and breadth of their country, are bored with antiquity and cannot see the necessity of uncovering still more old stones, as enthusiasts for archaeology do throughout Britain? Whatever the reason, one finds the professors at sites like the abandoned Etrusco-Roman city of Rusellae, a few miles north of Grosseto, working with no other help than that of local peasants hired to do the heavy digging. One will not see here those squads of amateurs, old and young, which one finds happily trowelling away at archaeological sites in Britain. Yet Rusellae, almost lost on its high hill and identifiable only by its great circle of Cyclopean walls undoubtedly built by the Etruscans and perhaps even before them, is one of the most beautiful and evocative places in Etruria, obviously needing several score of enthusiastic helpers working all through the spring and summer to lay bare the city that lies beneath the undergrowth which is just as impenetrable as it was when George Dennis visited the site a hundred and thirty years ago.

Yoked winged horses in terracotta, probably placed on the apex of a temple roof at Tarquinia. 5th–4th century B.C.

It is especially urgent that we overcome all the difficulties of finding experts, the enthusiasts to help them, and the time and money to explore in depth the scores of Etruscan places along the Tyrrhenian shore. Some of these locations are still only identifiable by their adjacent cemeteries. The Etruscans had their principal ports and emergency harbours along these shores, for we know from the volume of seaborne traffic that came into and went out of Etruria how vital they were to the economy. Ports like Pyrgi (Santa Marinella) and Alsium (Palo) were used by the inland cities of Caere and Veii, and Graviscae (now the Lido di Tarquinia) was an anchorage for Tarquinia. Ansedonia was the harbour serving Vulci and the neighbouring cities. Telamon and Populonia were other ports, and more anchorages probably reached up the coast perhaps as far as Genoa. It is these neglected or as yet unidentified sites which deserve further exploration, not so much to obtain additional museum exhibits, as to find out more about the economy and commerce of the pre-Roman period.

At present, the neglect of the ruins of such cities as Cosa, perched on its hill overlooking the Tyrrhenian Sea, means that the visitor can wander about inside the massive walls without knowing anything of the people who lived there, or even whether it was an Etruscan settlement before it became a Roman colony. Yet there is the evidence all around him, waiting to be examined by the archaeo-logists – the polygonal walls, the piles of masonry that rise up out of the scrub, and the deep pits which he would be wise to avoid. Cosa, which has been abandoned to cattle and birds and flowers, is, of course, a joy for those who wish to escape the rush of modern Italy. So perhaps it is fitting that this site, along with such beautiful places as Norchia, should remain undisturbed, a memorial to the people whose last earthly home it was.

Perhaps the end of this journey, which has purposely missed out the large cities and the usual tourist centres, should be Volterra, which can be reached by secondary roads either by going along the coast northwards from Cosa, or by turning inland at Follonica. The coast road will enable the explorer of minor Etruscan places to visit such sites as Telamon, one of the principal ports of this region of Etruria, though he should not expect to find any traces of the old harbour or of the docks and warehouses that must have grown up round it. These ancient ports were chiefly anchorages protected from the prevailing winds, and the ships that used them were shallow-draught galleys which did not need dredged channels or deep-water berths for unloading. But the remains of a temple, the existence of numerous tombs, and the discovery of an Etruscan city near by point to the importance of Telamon which was even entitled to mint its own coins.

Another and even more busy Etruscan harbour was Populonia, eighty miles to the north of Telamon, the Etruscan naval station from which the old sea kings dominated the sea lanes of the western Mediterranean. Indeed, Populonia was so important that the historian Livy includes it as one of the Twelve Cities

The Cyclopean walls of Rusellae, now being excavated by Italian archaeologists.

of the Etruscan league, and while this distinction (placing it alongside Tarquinia, Volterra, and Veii, and the other more famous cities of the Confederation) is questionable, there can be no doubt that a port within easy sailing distance of the islands of Elba, Sardinia, and Corsica was vital to the Etruscan economy. The proof of this has come to light in the recent excavations at Populonia, uncovering not only the remains of the city and its adjacent necropolis, but the immense deposits of slag thrown out from the iron smelting plants. In other words, after they had established commercial relations with Sardinia and Elba, the Etruscans organized the iron industry on an international scale, working the mines on the two offshore islands, importing the ore to Populonia on the mainland, smelting it on the spot, and exporting the pig iron to the eastern Mediterranean in exchange for those thousands of Greek vases which we find in the tombs. In addition, the port was undoubtedly used by the Etruscan fleet which in its heyday challenged the supremacy of both the Greek and the Carthaginian navies and which sent its warships as far east as the Greek islands, as far west as the coast of Spain, and possibly out into the Atlantic. So the Etruscans ruled the waves round the Italian coasts to the extent that two seas, the Tyrrhenian on the west and the Adriatic on the east, are named after them. Yet by the end of the first century B.C., when the Greek geographer Strabo visited Populonia, the residential part of the city was in ruins and the port itself was in disuse except for the tunny fishing fleets. Even this activity had ceased five hundred years later when the French traveller Rutilius, returning by ship from Rome, saw the ruins from the sea and wrote:

> Only the remnants of the broken walls remain;
> On every side the buildings lie scattered in ruins.[1]

And by the time George Dennis reached this rich emporium of Etruria, the place was a region of swamps and sand dunes, completely abandoned except for the shepherds, their flocks, and their fierce Abruzzi dogs which attacked the Englishman as he forced his way towards the site through the undergrowth. Dennis faced this hazard with characteristic calmness, reflecting on the advice of Pliny, who recommends sitting down on the ground if you are attacked by dogs, a procedure which Homer tells us worked for Odysseus confronted by the hounds of Eumaeus. Dennis did not emulate him, but preferred to retreat and continue his journey to Populonia by another route.

Turning inland from the coast, one travels north-eastwards towards Volterra across the hills which sweep away into the distance towards the still higher peaks of the Apennines. Each of the hills is crowned with its medieval town, and the loftiest of them all is Volterra which once commanded this whole region as far west as the sea coast where Populonia was its principal port and as far east as the mountains of the Italian spine. Volterra is the city where D. H. Lawrence finished his pilgrimage, and where we shall finish ours. We will find the town very much as he did, though it is almost fifty years since the English novelist with his American friend arrived in an ancient motor bus and was set down in front of the same hotel which his predecessor George Dennis calls the Unione, identified by its signboard portraying three naked females, presumably the three Graces. Dennis did not think much of the signboard, but recommends the hotel, which Lawrence in his turn found simple but comfortable. The hotel, now called the Nazionale, is still there, and could still be described in the same manner.

In fact, of all the larger Etruscan settlements that the traveller may visit, Volterra has changed the least since the first English explorers of Tuscany wrote about it for the Victorians, those omnivorous readers of guidebooks. The reason is partly its location in that region of Tuscany which is remote from the busy cities of the plains; Pisa to the north-west, Florence to the north-east, and Siena to the south east. It is also perched atop the highest hill of this near-mountainous country, and like the neighbouring small towns built by the Etruscans and fortified during the Middle Ages, it deliberately chose to remain cut off from the outside world for reasons of safety. There are dozens of such hill-top settlements in this region, all of them with their encirclement of walls, their

[1] Claudius Rutilius Namatianus, *Itinerarium sive de redito suo* (fifth century A.D.), I, 401–2.

watch towers, their ancient churches, narrow streets, and impressions of a secret life which the passing tourist can never penetrate and to which he can never belong. Volterra is like this, despite the concessions to modernity in the construction of new roads to enable the tourists to reach the famous museum in their cars. Otherwise, the town strikes the stranger in the 1970s as it struck Lawrence in the 1920s as 'peculiarly sombre and hard and resistant – it is no fun!'

Yet Volterra is unmistakably Etruscan, not only from the ruins of the walls and the surviving gates, but more from the views of the surrounding countryside, especially when the sun goes down in a blaze of gold. At such times it is not difficult to visualize the great Etruscan bastion of Velathri with its towers, temples, and palaces girded with a ring of walls five miles in circuit, the capital of the federation, with an empire larger than any other of the Twelve Cities. And in the museum where the treasures of the now lost or abandoned tombs are exhibited, one can finally meet Etruscans who belonged to the same breed of men as ourselves, not the mysterious denizens of the tombs or the mythical builders of Cyclopean walls or even the portly burghers laughed at by the Romans, but the ordinary people leaving on their journeys in covered wagons or in ships. We see them saying their last farewells to each other, husbands to wives, mothers to children. These portraits of their departure are symbolic of their passing into history, which is where we must leave them.

Frieze on an alabaster urn depicting a departure by covered wagon. A typical example of the rustic themes used by the old alabaster-sculptors of Volterra. 2nd century B.C.

Bibliography

Classical Sources

There are numerous references to the Etruscans in the works of the Greek and Roman historians, some specific, some generalized. The most factual information is found in the histories of the Greek writers *Herodotus* and *Dionysius of Halicarnassus*, though these two authorities disagree as to the provenance of the people the former calls 'Tyrrhenians' and the latter 'Rasenna'. The controversy has been going on ever since. The Roman authors *Livy* and *Pliny* have a great deal to say about the old rivals of Rome, though both writers were principally concerned with military history and wrote after the disappearance of Etruria as an imperial power. Etruscologists have sifted the evidence left by these and other ancient writers in the hope of finding some clue as to the provenance of the Etruscans, the nature of their institutions, and the origin of their language, but without much success. A complete list of ancient authors who mention the Etruscans will be found in Massimo Pallottino's *The Etruscans*.

General Histories

Banti, Luisa, *Il Mondo degli Etruschi*. Milan: Mondadori, 1960.

Bloch, Raymond, *The Etruscans*. Translated from the French by James Hogarth. London: Barrie and Rockliff, 1969.

Cameron, Mary Lovett, *Old Etruria and Modern Tuscany*. London: Methuen, 1969.

Dempster, Thomas, *De Etruria Regali Libri Septem*. Florence: Joannes Cajetanus Tartinius, 1723.

Ducati, Pericle, *Le Problème Étrusque*. Paris: Leroux, 1938.

Hampton, Christopher, *The Etruscans and the Survival of Etruria*. London: Gollancz, 1969.

Harrel-Courtès, Henry, *Etruscan Italy*, Translated from the French by James Hogarth. Edinburgh and London: Oliver & Boyd, 1964.

Harrel-Courtès, Henry, *L'Italie des Étrusques. Promenade au Pays des Ombres*. Paris: A. Michel, 1960.

Hergon, Jacques, *La Vie Quotidienne chez les Étrusques*. Paris: Gallimard, 1961.

Hus, Alain, *The Etruscans*. Translated from the French by Jeanne Unger Duell. New York: Grove Press, 1961.

Nogara, Bartolomeo, *Gli Etruschi e la Loro Civiltà*. Milan: U. Hoepli, 1932.

Pallottino, Massimo, *The Etruscans*. Translated from the Italian by J. Cremona. London: Penguin Books, 1955.

Pike, Edgar Royston, *Finding Out About the Etruscans*. London: Muller, 1964.

Richardson, Emeline Hill, *The Etruscans: their Art and Civilization*. Chicago: University of Chicago Press, 1964.

Solari, A., *La Vita Pubblica e Privata degli Etruschi*. Pisa: E. Spoerri, 1933.

Vacano, Otto Wilhelm von, *The Etruscans in the Ancient World*. Translated from the German by Sheila Ann Ogilvie. London: Arnold, 1960.

Vaughan, Agnes Carr, *These Mysterious Etruscans*. New York: Doubleday, 1966.

Explorers of Etruria

Burton, Sir Richard F., *Etruscan Bologna: a Study*. London: Smith & Elder, 1876.

Dennis, George, *The Cities and Cemeteries of Etruria*. London: Dent, Everyman's Library, 1907.
Dorow, Wilhelm, *Voyage Archaeologique dans l'Ancienne Étrurie*. Paris: Merlin, 1829.
Gell, Sir William, *Topography of Rome and its Vicinity*. London: H. Bohn, 1846.
Gray, Mrs Hamilton, *A Tour to the Sepulchres of Etruria in 1839*. London: Hatchard, 1843.

Special Studies
Beazley, J. D., 'The World of the Etruscan Mirror', in *The Journal of Hellenic Studies*, lxix, 1950.
Becq de Fouquières, L., *Les Jeux d'Anciens*, Paris: Reinwald, 1869.
Christie, James, *A Disquisition upon Etruscan Vases*. London: Longman, 1806.
Grenier, Albert, *Les Réligions Étrusque et Romaines*. Paris: Leroux, 1948.
Leland, Charles Godfrey, *Etruscan Roman remains in popular tradition*. London: Unwin, 1892.
Marcadé, Jean, *Roma-Amor*. Geneva: Nagel, 1961.
Moretti, Mario, *Nuovi Monumenti della Pitture Etrusca*. Milan: Lerici, 1966.
Pallottino, Massimo, *Art of the Etruscans*. London: Thames & Hudson, 1955.
Poulsen, P. R. S., *Etruscan Tomb Paintings*. London: Milford, 1922.
Radet, Georges, *La Lydie*. Paris: E. Thorin, 1893.
Reinach, S., *Repertoire des Vases Peints Grecs et Étrusques*. Paris: Leroux, 1922.
Riis, Poul Jorgen, *An Introduction to Etruscan Art*. Copenhagen: Borgens, 1953.
Taylor, Isaac, *Etruscan Researches*. London: Macmillan, 1874.
Weinstock, S., 'Martianus Capella and the Cosmic System of the Etruscans', *Journal of Roman Studies*, xxxvi, 1946.
Whatmough, Joshua, *The Foundations of Roman Italy*. London: Methuen, 1937.
Wolstenholme, G. E. W., and Cecilia M. O'Connor (editors), *The CIBA Symposium*. London: CIBA Foundation for the Promotion of International Cooperation in Medical and Chemical Research.

Language
Betham, Sir William, *Etruria-Celtica*. London: Groombridge, 1842.
Buonamici, Giulio, *Sul . . . la Questione della Lingua*. Faenza: published by the author, 1912.
Buonamici, Giulio, *Epigrafia Etrusca*. Florence: Institute of Etruscan Studies, 1932.
Carra de Vaux, Baron Bernard, *La Langue Étrusque: sa Place parmi les Langues*. Paris: G. Klincksiek, 1911.
Fowler, Murray, and R. G. Wolfe, *Materials for the Study of the Etruscan Language*. Madison: University of Wisconson Press, 1965.
Frengi, Giuseppe, *Delle più Celebre Inscrizione Etrusche*. Modena: A. Namias, 1897.
Geiger, Bernhard, *People and Languages of the Caucasus*. 's-Gravenhage: Mouton, 1959.
Guignard, Maurice, *Comment J'ai Déchiffré la Langue Étrusque*. Puttelange-lès-Thionville: published by the author, 1962.
Hempl, George, 'Early Etruscan Inscriptions', *The Matze Memorial Volume*. Stanford University Press, series No. 7, 1911.
Hilaire de Barenton, *La Texte Étrusque de la Mommie d'Agram*. Paris: Savaète & Maisonneuvè, 1929.
Krall, Jacob, 'Die Etruskischen Mumienbinder des Agramers Nationmuseums', *Akademie der Wissenschaften*, Bd.41. Vienna: F. Tempsky, 1892.
Lindsay, Alexander William, *Etruscan Inscriptions Analysed*. London: Longman, 1872.
Martha, Jules, *La Langue Étrusque*. Paris: Leroux, 1913.
Pauli, Carl, *Corpus Inscriptionum Etruscarum*. Rome, 1964.
Pei, Marius A., *The World's Chief Languages*. London: Allen & Unwin, 1949.
Taylor, Isaac, *The Etruscan Language*. London: Macmillan, 1876.
Trombetti, Alfredo, *La Lingua Etrusca*. Florence: Rinascimento del libro, 1928.

Notes on the Illustrations

Where the following abbreviations appear in the notes, they are intended to indicate the locations of pictures, and to acknowledge permission to reproduce photographs that the museums, art galleries and other institutions (or specifically their governing bodies) have granted in cases where they hold the copyright.

Guarnacci: Museo Guarnacci, Volterra. Louvre: Musée du Louvre, Paris. Mansell: The Mansell Collection, London. SAE: Soprintendenza alle Antichità d'Etruria, Florence. Villa Giulia: Museo di Villa Giulia, Rome. Vatican: Museo Gregoriano Etrusco, Vatican City State.

References to the books listed below have also been abbreviated.

Cities and Cemeteries: Cities and Cemeteries of Etruria by George Dennis. London: John Murray, 1948. *De Etruria: De Etruria Regali Libri Septem* by Thomas Dempster. Florence, 1723. *Etruria-Celtica: Etruria-Celtica* by Sir William Betham. London, 1842. *Hypogaei, or Sepulchral Caverns of Tarquinia* by James Byres. London, 1482. *Tour 1839: Tour to the Sepulchres of Etruria in 1839* by Mrs Hamilton Gray. London: Hatchard, 1841.

Jacket photos: Leonard von Matt (sculpture), Chris Ridley (background).

Reverse of frontispiece photo: Michael Holford Library.

Frontispiece photo: Leonard von Matt.

6 Photo: Mansell

10 Tomb, late 2nd century B.C. Photo: Leonard von Matt.

12 The National Trust, Sudbury Hall, Derbyshire. Photos: Studio 71.

13 *Cities and Cemeteries.* Photo: John Freeman.

14 Photo: Leonard von Matt.

15 By permission of Dennis Rhodes.

17 *Cities and Cemeteries.* Photo: John Freeman.

19 Photo: John Ross.

20 Antefixe found at Caere. Louvre. Photo: Giraudon.

22 Sarcophagus, 5th century B.C. Museo Archaeologico, Florence. Photo: SAE.

23 Photo: Mansell.

25 Photo: Alinari.

29 Photo: Michael Holford Library.

30–1 Jug, late 7th century B.C., found at Formella, near Veii. Villa Giulia. Photo: Scala.

32 Photo: Leonard von Matt.

34 Engraving from *Topography of Rome and its Vicinity* by William Gell, 1846. Photo: John Freeman.

35 Photo: Leonard von Matt.

36 *De Etruria.* Photos: John Freeman.

37 *Hypogaei.* Photo: John Freeman.

38–9 Urn, 2nd century B.C. Guarnacci. Photo: Leonard von Matt.

41 (Top) Musée des Beaux-Arts, Besançon. Photo: Giraudon. (Bottom) Sarcophagus found at Chiusi. Museo Archaeologico, Florence. Photo: Scala.

42 Photo: John Ross.

44 (Top) Frieze, 2nd century B.C. Guarnacci. Photo: Leonard von Matt. (Bottom) *De Etruria.* Photo: John Freeman.

46 Photo: Mansell.

47 Photos: Mansell.

48 *Hypogaei.* Photo: John Freeman.

49 (Top) *Hypogaei.* Photo: John Freeman. (Bottom) *Tour 1839.* Photo: John Freeman.

50–1 *Hypogaei.* Photos: John Freeman.

52 Lithograph by Delpech from a painting by Billiard. Photo: Mansell.

53 (Left) *Etruria-Celtica.* Photo: John Freeman. (Right) Ornament, 3rd century B.C. Photo: Leonard von Matt.

54 *Cities and Cemeteries.* Photo: John Freeman.

55 *Cities and Cemeteries.* Photo: John Freeman.

56 (Left) Vessel, late 8th century B.C., found at Cerveteri. Villa Giulia. Photo: Leonard von Matt. (Right) Bronze found at Vulci. British Museum.

57 Villa Giulia. Photo: Leonard von Matt.

59 Plate from *Auserlesene Griechische Vasenbilder hauptsachlich etruskischen Fundorts* by Edouard Gerhard, 1840–58. Photo: Library of Congress.

60 Villa Giulia. Photo: Leonard von Matt.

62–3 *Tour 1839.* Photos: John Freeman.

64–5 *Tour 1839.* Photos: John Freeman.

67 (Left) Jewellery, 7th century B.C., found in the Regolini Galassi Tomb at Caere. Photo: Alinari. (Right) By permission of Dennis Rhodes.

68 Museo Archaeologico, Chiusi. Photo: Leonard von Matt.

69 Photo: Mansell.

71–3 *Cities and Cemeteries*. Photos: John Freeman.

77 Villa Giulia. Photo: Leonard von Matt.

78 Photos: Leonard von Matt.

80 (Left) Oil painting by Jan Juta, 1920. National Portrait Gallery, London. (Right) Photo: Mansell.

81 *Etruria-Celtica*. Photos: John Freeman.

83 Sculpture, 2nd century B.C. Guarnacci. Photo: Leonard von Matt.

84 (Left) SAE. (Right) Ny Carlsberg Glyptothek, Copenhagen.

86–7 Museo Civico Archaeologico, Bologna.

88 Sculpture, 5th century B.C. British Museum. Photo: Mansell.

89 SAE.

90 *Cities and Cemeteries*. Photo: John Freeman.

91 Vase, mid-3rd century B.C. Photo: Alinari.

92 Frontispiece from *Memoire* by C. G. Leland. Photo: Library of Congress.

93 Museo Archaeologico, Orvieto. Photo: Mansell/Alinari.

95 Vatican. Photo: Scala.

96 Cista, late 4th century B.C., found at Praeneste. Villa Giulia. Photo: Leonard von Matt.

99 Frontispiece from *Gypsy Sorcery* by C. G. Leland. Photo: Library of Congress.

100 Engravings from *Etruscan Roman remains in popular tradition* by C. G. Leland, 1892. Photos: Library of Congress.

101 (Left) Photo: Stanford University Libraries. (Right) Oil painting by Thomas Eakins. American Philosophical Society.

102 Wall painting from the Tomb of Orcus, Tarquinia. Photo: Mansell/Anderson.

105 Photo: Leonard von Matt.

107 Wall painting, 4th century B.C. SAE.

108, 110–11 Cista, mid-4th century B.C., found at Praeneste. Villa Giulia. Photo: Leonard von Matt.

113 Cartographer: Ieuan Rees.

114 (Top) Coin, 4th century B.C. Photo: Leonard von Matt. (Middle and bottom) Photo: Mansell/Alinari.

115 Sarcophagus, 3rd century B.C. Guarnacci. Photo: Leonard von Matt.

116–17 (Left) Museo Archaeologico, Florence. Photo: Leonard von Matt. (Middle) Villa Giulia. Photo: Leonard von Matt. (Right) Villa Giulia. Photo: Leonard von Matt.

119 (Left and middle) Museum für Kunst und Gewerbe, Hamburg. (Right) Helmet found at Vulci. Photo: Mansell.

121 (Top) Villa Giulia. Photo: Michael Holford Library. (Bottom) Museo Communale, Cortona. Photo: John Ross.

122–3 Villa Giulia. Photo: Scala.

124 Villa Giulia. Photo: Scala.

126 Illustration from *Etruscan Cities and Rome*. Thames & Hudson, 1967. Photo: Fototeca Unione.

127 (Left) Metropolitan Museum of Art, New York. Fletcher Fund, 1932. (Right) Villa Giulia. Photo: Rainbird.

128–9 British Museum. Photo: Mansell.

131 Funerary stele in sandstone, 5th-4th century B.C. Museo Civico Archaeologico, Bologna.

133 Vessel, about 490 B.C., attributed to the 'Berlin' painter. British Museum. Photo: Michael Holford Library.

134 Photos: John Ross.

139 Mask, about 300 B.C. British Museum. Photo: Mansell.

140 (Left) Photo: Mansell. (Right) Antikensammlungen München.

141 Wall painting (reconstruction), about 310 B.C. Museo Archaeologico, Florence. Photo: Mansell/Alinari.

142 *Etruria-Celtica*. Photo: John Freeman.

142–3 Sculpture, about 500 B.C., found in Cyprus. Photo: Mansell.

143 *Etruria-Celtica*. Photo: John Freeman.

145 Mirror, early 5th century B.C. Vatican. Photo: Rainbird.

146–7 Bronze, 3rd century B.C., from Piacenza. Museo Civico, Piacenza. Photo: Scala.

148 Historisches Museum, Basel. Photo: John Ross.

149 Sculpture, 7th–6th century B.C. Antikensammlungen München.

151 Detail of sculpture, 6th–5th century B.C. Villa Giulia. Photo: Scala.

152 Photo: Leonard von Matt.

154 Vatican. Photo: Mansell/Alinari.

155 Villa Giulia. Photo: Scala.

156 Wall painting, about 530 B.C. Photo: Scala.

157 Villa Giulia. Photo: Leonard von Matt.

158 *Cities and Cemeteries*. Photo: John Freeman.

159 Bronze, 4th century B.C., found in the territory of Arezzo. Villa Giulia. Photo: Leonard von Matt.

161 (Top) Kylix by the Codrus painter. British Museum. Photo: Michael Holford Library. (Bottom) Amphora by the Eucharides painter. British Museum. Photo: Michael Holford Library.

162–3 Photo: Leonard von Matt.

164 Photo: Michael Holford Library.

167 Photo: Leonard von Matt.

168 *De Etruria*. Photo: John Freeman.

169 *Tour 1839*. Photo: John Freeman.

171 Calligraphy: Ieuan Rees.

173 SAE.

174–5 Photo: James Wellard.

176 Helmet, 474 B.C. British Museum.

177 (Left) British Museum. (Right) SAE.

179 Bibliothèque Nationale, Paris.

180–1 Sarcophagus, 3rd century B.C. Museo Nazionale Tarquiniense. Photo: Leonard von Matt.

183 (Left) Jug found at Viterbo. Metropolitan Museum of Art, New York. Fletcher Fund, 1924. (Right) Base of vase, 7th–6th century B.C., found at Cerveteri. Vatican. Photo: Anderson.

184 (Left) Vatican. Photo: Anderson. (Right) Villa Giulia. Photo: Leonard von Matt.

186 *Etruria-Celtica*. Photos: John Freeman.

189 and jacket back Villa Giulia. Photo: Scala.

190 Villa Giulia. Photo: John Ross.

193 Photo: Mansell/Alinari.

195 Bronze, late 5th century B.C. Photo: Leonard von Matt.

196 Bronze, 2nd century B.C. Villa Giulia. Photo: Leonard von Matt.

197 Photo: Mansell/Alinari.

198–9 *Cities and Cemeteries*. Photo: John Freeman.

200 *Tour 1839*. Photo: John Freeman.

201 Detail of a wall painting, about 450 B.C. Photo: Fotoedizioni Sacco, Chiusi.

203 Photo: Mansell/Alinari.

204 Museo Nazionale Archaeologico, Palermo. Photo: Leonard von Matt.

207 Bronzes, 5th century B.C., from Cagli, Villa Giulia. Photo: Leonard von Matt.

208 Photo: Scala.

211 Photo: Fototeca Unione, Rome.

213 Photo: Leonard von Matt.

Endpapers Soprintendenza alle Antichità, Palermo. Illustration from *Arms and Armour of the Greeks*. Thames & Hudson, 1967.

Index

Page numbers given in *italics* refer to illustrations.